MAX notes

Charles Dickens'

A Tale of Two Cities

Text by
Jeffrey Karnicky
B.A., Rutgers University

Dr. M. Fogiel
Chief Editor

Illustrations by
Michael A. Kupka

Research & Education Association

MAXnotes™ for
A TALE OF TWO CITIES

Printed in the United States of America

Library of Congress Catalog Card Number 94-65957

International Standard Book Number 0-87891-949-X

MAXnotes™ is a trademark of
Research & Education Association, Piscataway, New Jersey 08854

What **MAXnotes**™ *Will Do for You*

This book is intended to help you absorb the essential contents and features of Charles Dickens' *A Tale of Two Cities* and to help you gain a thorough understanding of the work. The book has been designed to do this more quickly and effectively than any other study guide.

For best results, this **MAXnotes** book should be used as a companion to the actual work, not instead of it. The interaction between the two will greatly benefit you.

To help you in your studies, this book presents the most up-to-date interpretations of every section of the actual work, followed by questions and fully explained answers that will enable you to analyze the material critically. The questions also will help you to test your understanding of the work and will prepare you for discussions and exams.

Meaningful illustrations are included to further enhance your understanding and enjoyment of the literary work. The illustrations are designed to place you into the mood and spirit of the work's settings.

The **MAXnotes** also include summaries, character lists, explanations of plot, and chapter-by-chapter analyses. A biography of the author and discussion of the work's historical context will help you put this literary piece into the proper perspective of what is taking place.

The use of this study guide will save you the hours of preparation time that would ordinarily be required to arrive at a complete grasp of this work of literature. You will be well-prepared for classroom discussions, homework, and exams. The guidelines that are included for writing papers and reports on various topics will prepare you for any added work which may be assigned.

The **MAXnotes** will take your grades "to the max."

— Dr. Max Fogiel
Program Director

Contents

> **Each chapter includes List of Characters, Summary, Analysis, Study Questions and Answers, and Suggested Essay Topics.**

Introduction

The Life and Work of Charles Dickens

Charles Dickens was born in Portsmouth, England, on February 7, 1812. His family moved to London in 1821, where Dickens' father became overwhelmed by debt, ending up in debtors' prison. Charles was forced to take a factory job at the age of 12. This first-hand experience with poverty informs much of his later writings. Dickens escaped from this world of debt, thanks to the help of some relatives who made it possible for him to get a formal education at the Wellington House Academy.

In 1834, Dickens took a job as a reporter for *The Morning Chronicle*; he also began publishing various sketches and essays in periodicals. Some of this early work was reprinted as *Sketches by Boz* (1836). With the serial publication of *The Pickwick Papers* in the same year, Dickens became one of the most popular authors of his time. In the midst of this sudden success, Dickens married Catherine Hogarth. The marriage was an unhappy one, finally ending in separation 23 years later.

The success of *The Pickwick Papers* was followed by the serial publication of *Oliver Twist* (1837), *Nicholas Nickleby* (1838-9), *The Old Curiousity Shop* (1840-1), and Dickens' first historical novel, *Barnaby Rudge* (1841). All of these works sold remarkably well. Dickens traveled in America for the next year, returning with *American Notes* (1842) and *A Christmas Carol* (1843). Dickens spent the next few years traveling in Europe.

The autobiographical *David Copperfield* (1849-50) began a series of more serious novels, including *Bleak House* (1852-3) and *Hard Times* (1854), with more structured plots that directly criticized his society and government. Following the separation from his wife in 1858, Dickens published *A Tale of Two Cities* (1859), an historical novel dealing with the French Revolution. While working on the never-to-be-completed novel *The Mystery of Edwin Drood*, Dickens suffered two strokes. This second stroke led directly to his death on June 9, 1870.

Historical Background

Charles Dickens was the most popular English novelist of the Victorian Age, a time period spanning roughly from the 1820s to the end of the nineteenth century. While the revolutions in America and France had happened many years earlier, there was still great social tension in England during these times. Work conditions for the poor were horrid, often resulting in strikes that ended in violent clashes between the police and the workers.

A Tale of Two Cities can be seen as a warning to British society of the mid-nineteenth century. Dickens calls attention to the extraordinary violence of the French Revolution, while showing that the overthrow of a government by violent means inevitably leads to more killing. Many revolutionaries of his day failed to see that Dickens was more concerned with portraying the death and destruction that accompany revolution than with endorsing a working class revolt.

Indeed, Dickens' popularity crossed all class lines. His writings were as much a topic of upper-class drawing room party conversation, as they were among the factory workers who could afford to buy the weekly serializations.

Critics were only slightly less kind to Dickens. While he was sometimes faulted for sentimentality and for relying on unbelievable plot coincidences, he was more often celebrated for his ability to create characters who seem alive and who embody a moral principle. Writers in the 1800s were looked to as moral examples, and Charles Dickens was not short on morality in his novels.

Master List of Characters

Jarvis Lorry—*a lifelong bachelor and clerk at Tellson's Bank, as well as a friend of the Manette's and of Charles Darnay.*

Lucie Manette—*the daughter of Alexandre Manette. She marries Charles Darnay.*

Dr. Alexandre Manette—*Lucie's father. At the novel's beginning he is freed from 18 years of imprisonment.*

Charles Darnay—*a self-exiled member of French ruling class society, also known as Charles Evremonde. He marries Lucie Manette, returns to France, and is sentenced to die.*

Ernest Defarge—*owns a wine-shop in a Paris suburb. Along with his wife, he is a leader of the revolt in Paris.*

Therese Defarge—*the wife of Defarge and the co-leader of revolt. She knits names of those to be killed when the revolution comes.*

Sydney Carton—*the physical double of Charles Darnay who secretly does Stryver's legal work. He heroically dies in place of Darnay.*

Mr. Stryver—*a lawyer who defends Darnay in England. He wants to marry Lucie Manette.*

Jerry Cruncher—*valet and personal messenger for Jarvis Lorry.*

Miss Pross—*Lucie Manette's dedicated servant. She struggles with and kills Madame Defarge.*

Monsieur the Marquis—*French nobleman killed by a peasant. He is also the uncle of Charles Darnay.*

Monsieur Gabelle—*the Marquis' servant who later summons Charles Darnay to England.*

John Barsad—a spy who is also known as Solomon Pross, Miss Pross' brother.

Roger Cly—*he is sentenced to death as a spy in England.*

Foulon—*Foulon is a French nobleman killed during the revolution.*

The Vengeance, the mender of roads/wood-sawyer, and various "Jacques"—*various followers of the Defarges who participate in the revolt in Paris.*

A tall man in a nightcap—*his baby is killed by the Marquis' coach. He murders the Marquis and is guillotined.*

Mrs. Jerry Cruncher—*Jerry Cruncher's wife.*

Master Jerry Cruncher—*the son of Jerry Cruncher.*

Little Lucie Manette—*the daughter of Lucie Manette and Charles Darnay.*

Woman going to guillotine—*she talks with Sydney Carton as they await their deaths.*

Summary of the Novel

A Tale of Two Cities is concerned with events in Paris and London before and during the French Revolution. The story focuses on Charles Darnay, the self-exiled nephew of French nobility, and his wife, Lucie Manette, daughter of Dr. Alexandre Manette. As the first of the novel's three sections begins, Jarvis Lorry is on his way to Paris to reunite Dr. Manette with the daughter who thought he has been dead for the past 18 years. Over this time Dr. Manette has forgotten his past life; he sits in a small attic room and makes shoes. Slowly, Jarvis and Lucie Manette "recall (him) to life."

The novel's second section starts five years later. Lucie Manette marries Charles Darnay. Darnay confesses a secret to Dr. Manette on the eve of the wedding. This secret turns out to be that Darnay is really Charles Evremonde, a member of the French ruling class. Darnay has renounced his past and wishes to settle in England. Meanwhile, unrest is growing in the Paris suburb of St. Antoine. The center of this unrest is a wine-shop owned by the Defarges, who are shown leading the storming of the Bastille.

The final section of the novel opens with Darnay on his way to Paris at the entreaty of a former servant who is endangered. Darnay is arrested and sentenced to die. The Manettes and Lorry hurry to Paris and succeed in freeing Darnay, but he is soon arrested again. He is sentenced to the guillotine. Sydney Carton, who bears a striking resemblance to Darnay, sneaks into the prison and switches places with Darnay. Carton is on his way to the guillotine, willing to die for the love of Lucie, while Darnay, the Manettes and Lorry flee to London.

Estimated Reading Time

Like most Victorian authors, Dickens could be verbose. At roughly 400 pages, *A Tale of Two Cities* is actually one of his shorter novels. While the optimal way to read this novel would be to read one weekly installment at a time, this is impractical. As the novel is broken into three sections, a better reading plan would be to read the first section in one sitting, while devoting two sittings each to the final two longer sections. Total reading time should be approximately 12 hours.

Book the First: Recalled to Life

Chapter 1: The Period
Chapter 2: The Mail
Chapter 3: The Night Shadows

New Characters:

Jerry Cruncher: *messenger who becomes valet and personal messenger for Jarvis Lorry*

Jarvis Lorry: *lifelong bachelor and clerk at Tellson's Bank; he is a friend of the Manette's and Charles Darnay*

Summary

The year is 1775. France is described as on the verge of revolution; England is said to be "scarcely" better. A coach is taking the mail to Dover. Jarvis Lorry is a passenger on this coach. It is late at night, and a horse is heard approaching at a quick pace. The passengers and driver fear that it is a highwayman. The coach stops; the coachman threatens to shoot the man approaching on horseback.

But it is only Jerry Cruncher with a message for Jarvis Lorry from Tellson's Bank: "Wait at Dover for Mam'selle." Lorry gives a

message for Jerry to return with– "RECALLED TO LIFE." The narrator reflects on the idea that every person is "a profound secret and mystery to every other." Jarvis Lorry dozes, and dreams of a conversation with a man who was "buried…almost eighteen years." Lorry raises the window shade and sees that the sun has risen.

Analysis

These opening chapters set up a parallel between London and Paris in the 1750s. Dickens' famous opening line "It was the best of times, it was the worst of times…" draws another parallel with the 1850s, his time, when *A Tale of Two Cities* was published. This allows Dickens to develop two themes throughout the novel: first, that no historical period will ever be without serious problems, and, second, that violence is not the best answer to societal problems. The coachman's threat to Jerry Cruncher personifies humankind's willingness to judge others quickly and harshly. The mysterious mention of the buried person without further explanation is an example of the way in which Dickens uses suspense to prod his reader on to the next chapter.

Study Questions

1. What are the two cities of the novel's title?

2. What purpose does the comparison of England and France serve?

3. What further comparison is implied by the connection of England and France?

4. Why is the coachman nervous when he hears a horse approaching?

5. What is the man on horseback's true purpose, and what exchange takes place?

6. What does the narrator reflect upon concerning humankind?

7. For how long has the man in Jarvis Lorry's thoughts been buried?

8. What else do we know of this man who has been "buried"?

9. Why is this all of the information the reader has on this subject?

10. How does this scene end?

Answers

1. The two cities are Paris and London.

2. It serves to show that people are very similar, no matter where they are.

3. This connection makes the larger point that Dickens' readers are not much different from people during the time of the French Revolution.

4. The coachman fears that it may be a highwayman wanting to rob them.

5. He has a message for Jarvis Lorry: "Wait at Dover for Mam'selle." Lorry, in return, gives him the message: "RE-CALLED TO LIFE."

6. The narrator reflects on the fact that no person can really know another person.

7. He has been buried for 18 years.

8. We know nothing else of this man.

9. This is all the information that the author supplies in order to build suspense so that the reader will continue reading.

10. The scene ends with Jarvis Lorry looking out the coach window to see the sun rising.

Suggested Essay Topics

1. Discuss the theme of the likeness of people despite differences of place or time. Is this relationship useful only within the context of *A Tale of Two Cities*, or can it be applied to other situations?

2. How does the fear of the messenger illustrate the narrator's idea that it is impossible to know another person? Does anything else in these opening chapters support this thought? Does anything contradict it?

Chapter 4: The Preparation

New Character:

Lucie Manette: *daughter of Alexandre Manette*

The mail safely arrives at Dover; Jarvis Lorry is the only passenger left on the coach, the two other passengers having been dropped off earlier. Lorry checks into the Royal George Hotel, has a haircut, eats breakfast, and takes a nap. Upon waking, he reserves a room for a young woman he is expecting to meet there. He meets this woman, Lucie Manette, and we learn that he is to accompany her to France to settle some business concerning property of her father.

Miss Manette believes that her father is dead. Lorry tries to tell her gently that her father is not dead. He begins to tell her the story of a man who had not died, but disappeared; Lucie realizes that this man is her father. She is overwhelmed and grabs hold of Lorry's wrists. This makes Lorry nervous and he insists that she calm down, since they are conducting business. Lucie exclaims, "I am going to see his ghost." Lorry tells Lucie that her father has lost his memory and that he must be spirited out of France. Lucie becomes insensibly silent until her servant, Miss Pross, enters and calms her.

Analysis

In this chapter, the plot connection between England and France is formed. Jarvis Lorry has worked for Tellson's Bank in both London and Paris, and the Manettes are originally from France. We find out that Alexandre Manette is the man who has been in prison for the past 18 years, but the suspense is not lessened. Lorry states that Dr. Manette must be secretly removed from France, and that he has lost his memory. Both of these plot devices keep the reader interested in reading more.

The reader learns of Mr. Lorry's lifelong dedication to his work, suggesting that one who is so industrious does not have time for a wife. Lorry can be seen as representing organization, frugality, and self-sacrifice throughout the novel, even as he comes to befriend the Manettes.

Lucie Manette is portrayed as a weak woman, incapable of doing anything. She is idealized and will later be contrasted with the evil Madame Defarge. This Victorian portrayal of the ideal woman as passive and reliant on men is problematic and warrants further discussion.

Study Questions

1. What does Mr. Lorry do upon arrival in Dover?

2. Whom does Lorry meet here, and what plans do they make?

3. How does Lorry begin to tell Lucie that her father is not dead?

4. Why does he employ this method?

5. Why does Lorry insist to Lucie that all of his relations are mere business relations?

6. What does Lucie say upon learning that she is going to see her father?

7. What are the two conditions concerning Dr. Manette?

8. What is Lucie's reaction to this?

9. Who comes into the room at this point to help Lucie?

10. What is problematic about this portrayal of Lucie Manette?

Answers

1. He checks into the Royal George Hotel and takes a nap.

2. Lorry meets Lucie Manette here, and they make plans to go to France concerning some property of her father. Since she thinks she is an orphan, she has asked the bank to provide her with an escort.

3. He begins to tell her the "story" of a man like her father, who did not die 18 years ago, but was imprisoned.

4. He fears that telling her that her father is alive may be more than she can handle.

5. She has grabbed his wrists in her fear. Lorry does not want to get personally involved; as a model of organization and frugality, he must keep his distance.

6. She says, "I am going to see his ghost! It will be his ghost—not him!"

7. First, that he has lost his memory of any past life. Second, that he must be removed from France in secret.

8. She sits silently in her chair, unable to utter a word.

9. Her servant, Miss Pross, enters and calms Lucie.

10. Lucie is portrayed as unable to take care of herself. She will constantly be defined in terms of her reliance on others.

Suggested Essay Topics

1. Write an essay reflecting on Mr. Lorry's insistence that all of his relations are of the business type. Why could this be im-

portant as to what his character represents? How is this related to his lifelong bachelorhood? How does this reflect the Victorian Age?

2. Write an essay discussing the way Lucie Manette is portrayed as a woman in this chapter. What problems arise from this depiction? Is this a mere reflection of Victorian ideals, or is it relevant to today's times?

Chapter 5: The Wine-Shop

New Characters:

Ernest Defarge: *owner of wine-shop in Paris suburb; along with wife, a leader of the revolt in Paris*

Therese Defarge: *wife of Ernest Defarge and co-leader of the revolt; she knits the names of those to be killed when the revolution comes*

The three "Jacques": *followers of the Defarges who participate in the revolt in Paris*

Dr. Alexandre Manette: *Lucie's father who is freed after 18 years in a French prison*

Summary

The scene is a street in the Paris suburb of Saint Antoine. A cask of red wine has been dropped and broken. All of the people in the area, businessmen and idlers alike, have stopped what they are doing and are drinking the spilled wine. Many faces and hands have become stained red. A man writes "BLOOD" on a wall.

St. Antoine is described as a gloomy town, full of "cold, dark, sickness, ignorant, and want." The wine-shop is said to be of a slightly better standard than most businesses in St. Antoine. Ernest Defarge, the owner of the wine-shop, is a "man of strong resolution and set purpose." His wife sits inside the wine-shop, knitting. Three customers in the wine-shop have a conversation with Defarge about the spilt wine. Defarge refers to all three men as "Jacques." Defarge directs the three "Jacques" to a bachelor

apartment that they wish to see. In reality, he is directing them to the room where Dr. Manette is.

Mr. Lorry and Lucie, who have been sitting quietly in the corner, now approach Defarge. Defarge leads the two of them up a staircase; they pass the three "Jacques" on the way. We learn that Dr. Manette is in a locked room, above the wine-shop, and that Defarge shows him to people on occasion.

Lorry leads Lucie into the room, murmuring of "business, business!" She is afraid of her father and again clutches Lorry. The room is dark; Dr. Manette is stooped over a bench, making shoes.

Analysis

The spilt wine is a foreshadowing of the bloodshed to come. This is made obvious by the peasant who writes "BLOOD" on the wall, and when the narrator says "the time was to come, when that wine too would be spilled on the street-stones, and when the stain of it would be red upon many there." We see that the Paris suburbs are full of disgruntled people living in virtual squalor; these are the very masses that will provide the manpower for the coming revolution. The single-mindedness of the crowd anticipates the mob logic that leads to much more violence later in the novel. The power and horror of crowds is one of the major themes in *A Tale of Two Cities.*

The use of the name "Jacques" comes from the ruling class' dismissal of all members of the lower class as so many "Jacques." The peasants empower themselves by adopting the term and referring to their cohorts in revolutionary thought as "Jacques." Defarge shows the "Jacques" Dr. Manette because he thinks it will help the revolutionary cause by letting people know that Dr. Manette was a prisoner of the nobility.

Once again we see the weak nature of Lucie Manette when she has to cling to Lorry. Madame Defarge is barely sketched out in this chapter, but already there are ominous overtones to her character. She is "stout," with "large hands," and "a watchful eye." In other words, she does not fit the Victorian ideal of a fragile, docile woman.

Study Questions

1. What is happening at the beginning of this chapter?
2. What does the man write on the wall? What does this foreshadow?
3. What kind of town is Saint Antoine?
4. Who are the proprietors of the wine-shop?
5. What is the significance of the name "Jacques"?
6. What is the impression of Madame Defarge from this chapter?
7. Why does Defarge show Dr. Manette to the "Jacques"?
8. Where is Dr. Manette being held?
9. What is Lucie's reaction upon seeing him?
10. What is Dr. Manette doing when they enter his room?

Answers

1. A cask of wine has broken open on the street of a Paris suburb. All of the townspeople are engaged in drinking the wine and staining themselves with its red color.
2. He writes "BLOOD." This anticipates the real blood that will be spilled in the name of revolution.
3. Saint Antoine is described as a place full of "cold, dark, sickness, ignorance, and want."
4. The proprietors of the wine-shop are Ernest and Therese Defarge.
5. The peasants adopted this name from what the nobility called them. They turned a derogatory name into one that helped give them a sense of common purpose.
6. She is "stout" and ominous; she can be seen as the polar opposite of the diffident Lucie Manette.

7. He feels that Dr. Manette is a symbol of the cruelty of the ruling class.

8. He is being held in a tiny, dark room in an apartment above the wine-shop.

9. She is scared and reaches to Mr. Lorry for comfort.

10. He is bent over a bench, making shoes.

Suggested Essay Topics

1. How does this chapter foreshadow the coming revolution? Look beyond the obvious answer that equates the wine with blood. What does the single-mindedness of the crowd mean in this context? What of the desolate conditions that they live in?

2. Discuss the significance of the name "Jacques." What do the peasants gain by addressing each other in this way? How did they come to use this term? Discuss any contemporary manifestations of this idea.

Chapter 6: The Shoemaker

Summary

Dr. Manette is a feeble old man, nearly destroyed by physical weakness. Defarge wants to let more light into the room, and the old man is indifferent. Dr. Manette tells them that he is making "a young ladies walking-shoe." When they ask him his name, he replies "One Hundred and Five, North Tower." Dr. Manette returns to the shoe. He slowly begins to recall his daughter and Mr. Lorry. Lucie holds him and kisses him, and he remembers her and makes an impassioned speech. It is decided that they should leave for England immediately. Mr. Lorry makes another reference to "business." As they are leaving, Lorry says to Dr. Manette, "I hope you care to be recalled to life?" to which Dr. Manette replies, "I can't say." This is the end of the first section of the novel.

Analysis

In this chapter we see the terrible nature of what a long imprisonment can do to a man. His reciting of his cell number, "One Hundred and Five, North Tower," when asked his name shows the extent to which prison has robbed him of his identity. This point is further emphasized by the fact that he is making shoes and has forgotten that he is a doctor.

We also see what is supposed to be the strength of Lucie, that is, her power to restore her father's memory through love, hugs, and kisses. Dr. Manette is overcome by emotion on hearing his daughter's voice. Her love for him apparently gives him the power to remember his past.

Mr. Lorry's insistence that he is merely doing "business" is repeated once again, perhaps suggesting that he is beginning to feel a personal attachment to the Manettes, but is unwilling to admit this to himself.

This chapter once again ends on a suspenseful note, with the reader unsure if Dr. Manette will ever be "recalled to life."

Study Questions

1. What is Dr. Manette's condition?

2. What does Dr. Manette say his name is?

3. What is the significance of what he says?

4. What helps Dr. Manette begin to remember his past?

5. How soon do they decide to leave France?

6. Why does Mr. Lorry refer to "business" again?

7. What is Lucie's "strength" in this chapter?

8. What is the importance of Dr. Manette returning to the shoe he is making?

9. What does Mr. Lorry say to Dr. Manette?

10. What is the nature of Dr. Manette's reply? What function does his reply serve regarding the plot?

Answers

1. Dr. Manette is weak and feeble. He cannot remember his past; he cannot even remember his name.

2. He says "One Hundred and Five, North Tower."

3. This is the number of his prison cell and an illustration of how his long imprisonment has stolen his identity.

4. Lucie shows that she loves him by showering him with affection.

5. They decide to leave France immediately.

6. He refers to "business" because he may be trying to deny that he is forming a personal connection with the Manettes.

7. Her strength is that her love is able to do good—for instance, helping her father remember his past.

8. This shows that he has a long way to go in recalling his past as a doctor.

9. Mr. Lorry asks Dr. Manette, "I hope you care to be recalled to life?"

10. Dr. Manette replies, "I can't say." This leaves the plot dangling, urging the reader on to the next installment.

Suggested Essay Topics

1. Write an essay exploring the ways in which Dr. Manette has lost his identity. Use specific examples to show how much of his past he has forgotten.

2. Discuss the role of Lucie's affections in helping her father remember his past. Does this present any problems in a contemporary context? How does this help to define Lucie as a character? What does this say about the role of women in Victorian society?

Book the Second:
The Golden Thread

Chapter 1: Five Years Later
Chapter 2: A Sight

New Characters:

Mrs. Jerry Cruncher: *wife of Jerry Cruncher*

Master Jerry Cruncher: *son of Jerry Cruncher*

Charles Darnay (a.k.a. Charles Evremonde): *self-exiled member of French ruling class society*

Members of the British Court: *the spectators, the judge, and the attorney-general who is prosecuting Darnay*

Summary

Five years have passed since the end of the first section of the novel. Tellson's Bank is described as an old-fashioned place, proud of its smallness, darkness, and ugliness. We learn that the death penalty was put to great use in England in 1780 for such minor crimes as forgery and petty theft.

Jerry Cruncher is sitting outside Tellson's Bank, waiting to be appointed an errand to run. His 12-year-old son waits with him.

The scene then shifts to the Crunchers' small apartment, in a bad neighborhood. Mr. Cruncher argues with his wife; she claims that she is praying, and he complains that she is praying against him. Mr. Cruncher calls his wife a "conceited female" and asks her what she thinks her prayers are worth. She replies, "They only come from the heart, Jerry. They are worth no more than that." Mr. Cruncher and his son, who are said to look extremely like each other, go off to Tellson's Bank. A porter is called for, and the elder Cruncher is off, leaving young Jerry to contemplate why his father's fingers are always rusty.

Cruncher's job is to go to the Old Bailey, which is the court, and wait there for instructions from Mr. Lorry. Cruncher finds out that a man is on trial for treason. Cruncher meets a man at the court who is excited about the prospects of seeing the defendant in the treason case drawn and quartered "when" he is found guilty.

Cruncher asks if he means "if" they find him guilty. The man replies, "Oh! They'll find him guilty."

The man on trial is Charles Darnay. He is described as 25, "well-grown, and well-looking." The crowd in the courtroom cannot wait to see this man put to a public death. Dr. and Lucie Manette are in the courtroom. Lucie is described as full of compassion for the prisoner, "a compassion that saw nothing but the peril of the accused." She sits close to her father in her fear. The crowd begins to ask "Who are they?" We learn that Lucie and Dr. Manette are witnesses against the prisoner.

Analysis

Jerry Cruncher provides a comic element to the plot. We are confronted with the mystery of why he has rust on his hands all of the time, a question that will tie in later with the main plot. It is a Dickens' trademark to have all of his subplots integrate with the main plot line in a nearly unbelievable way by the end of the story.

Cruncher and his son are described as very much alike, perhaps to show that it is impossible for young Jerry ever to be anything besides what his father is, an illustration of the rigidity of social class.

The scene in the courtroom shows that when crowds lose their sense of identity, they can also lose all sense of responsibility and compassion. Their desire to see Darnay publicly executed illustrates this. The remark that they will find Darnay guilty reflects on the idea that justice in England in 1780 was anything but fair to the defendant.

Lucie Manette is seen in direct opposition to the crowd; she is full of feminine compassion for Darnay. This compassion is again said to be her great strength, even though she is so physically fragile that she has to hold tightly to her father. The revelation that Dr. Manette and Lucie are witnesses against Darnay, despite their compassion for him, once again ends a chapter on a suspenseful note.

Study Questions

1. How is Tellson's Bank described at the beginning of the chapter?

2. What is the eighteenth century view of the death penalty in England?

3.   Why does Jerry Cruncher call his wife "a conceited female," and what is her reaction to this?

4.   What is the significance of the striking physical resemblance between Jerry Cruncher and his son?

5.   Why is there such a large crowd in the courtroom?

6.   What does Jerry Cruncher ask the man who assumes that Darnay will be found guilty?

7.   Why do all eyes in the courtroom turn to Lucie Manette?

8.   How is Lucie Manette different from those around her in the courtroom?

9.   How is this strength undermined?

10. On what suspenseful note does the chapter end?

Answers

1.   Tellson's Bank is an unchanging, old-fashioned place, proud of its dirtiness and ugliness.

2.   The death penalty was in great use for even minor crimes.

3.   He calls her conceited because he assumes that she thinks her prayers are worth something. She tells him that the prayers come from her heart, and that is all that they are worth.

4.   This shows that young Jerry will probably end up just like his father, stuck rigidly in a low social class.

5.   The crowd is large because many people wish to see a public execution.

6.   He asks this man if he means "if" they find the defendant guilty. The man assures Cruncher that the jury will find him guilty.

7.   All eyes turn to her because of the striking expression of fear and compassion on her face.

8.   She is one of the few people in the courtroom who are able to feel pity for the prisoner.

9. Her moral strength is undermined by her physical weakness, shown by her need to cling to her father.

10. We learn that, although Lucie feels compassion for the prisoner, she is a witness against him.

Suggested Essay Topics

1. Write an essay describing how Dickens portrays the English court system of the 1780s. Pay attention to the discussion of the death penalty, the conversation between Jerry Cruncher and the man who wishes to see Darnay drawn and quartered, and the nature of the crowd in the courtroom.

2. Write an essay comparing the behavior of Lucie Manette and Mrs. Cruncher in these chapters. What do these two women have in common? Is their class difference more important than their similarities, as portrayed by Dickens?

Chapter 3: A Disappointment

New Characters:

Mr. Stryver: *lawyer who defends Darnay in England; he wants to marry Lucie Manette*

John Barsad: *a spy also known as Solomon Pross; Miss Pross' brother*

Roger Cly: *killed as a spy in England*

Sydney Carton: *physical double of Charles Darnay who secretly does Stryver's legal work*

Summary

The Attorney-General tells the jury that the prisoner has been conducting secret business between France and England for at least five years. He describes, in glowing terms, a patriot who has figured out the devious nature of the spy. A second witness, the prisoner's servant, will present some papers that will condemn the prisoner. The first witness, John Barsad, is called. Upon cross-ex-

amination by Mr. Stryver, it becomes known that Barsad has been in debtor's prison and that he owes the prisoner money. Roger Cly, the prisoner's servant, is revealed to have known Barsad for seven or eight years. The papers that Cly says are the prisoner's cannot be proven to be in the prisoner's handwriting.

The prosecution builds its case around the fact that five years ago Lucie Manette talked with Darnay on a boat going from France to England. She says that Darnay told her he was traveling under an assumed name because of the sensitive nature of what he must do.

The prosecution has a witness who insists that he can identify and incriminate Darnay. Just at this point, Mr. Stryver draws the court's attention to Sydney Carton, a man who bears a striking physical resemblance to Darnay. Lucie nearly faints; the jury acquits Darnay on the grounds that mistakes of identification can easily be made. Darnay apologizes to Lucie. Barsad and Cly are exposed as swindlers. The crowd leaving the courtroom is described as "dispersing in search of other carrion."

Analysis

Dickens uses comedy to make a serious point in this chapter. The Attorney-General describes his witnesses in a way that is antithetical to their true nature. This outright lying nearly leads to a conviction until the unbelievable coincidence of the look-alike is revealed. This reliance on coincidence in plot is one of the chief criticisms of Dickens as a novelist.

Lucie Manette is once again shown to be physically weak in her heroism, while at the same time, a hint of her affection for Darnay is revealed.

Dickens builds more suspense by never addressing just exactly what Darnay was doing traveling secretly between England and France, if he was not a traitor. This suspense continues for many more chapters.

The mob mentality grows more ominous in this chapter, foreshadowing the revolution in France, as the dispersing crowd is described as needing to find a release for their need to see death.

Study Questions

1. What does the Attorney-General say about the prisoner in his opening statements?

2. Who are the two witnesses that the Attorney-General says will incriminate Darnay?

3. How does Stryver show that these two men are not credible witnesses?

4. Why is Lucie Manette called to the witness stand?

5. What did Darnay tell Lucie on the ship five years ago?

6. What leads to Darnay's acquittal?

7. What problem concerning Dickens' use of plot does this reveal?

8. What happens to Lucie Manette, once again, in this chapter?

9. What is the final line of this chapter?

10. What are the implications of this line?

Answers

1. He says that the prisoner has been engaged in secret business between France and England for at least the past five years.

2. One is described as a patriot who has been able to figure out what the prisoner has been doing; his name is John Barsad. The other is the prisoner's former servant, Roger Cly.

3. He shows that Barsad has been in debtors' prison and that he owes the prisoner money. Stryver proves that Cly is a thief who has been friends with Barsad for many years.

4. She is called to the witness stand because she talked to Darnay on a boat ride from France to England five years before.

5. He told her that he was conducting business of a sensitive nature and that he was traveling under an assumed name.

6. A man who looks exactly like Darnay proves to the jury that it is very easy to mistake one person for another.

7. This plot twist is too coincidental to be believable.

8. Her physical strength fails her when she feels strong emotions.

9. The crowd is described as "dispersing in search of other carrion."

10. This line implies that a crowd can easily develop a lust for violence that has little to do with justice.

Suggested Essay Topics

1. Write an essay exploring the use of comedy in this chapter. Contrast the ways in which the prosecution and the defense portray the witnesses. Discuss the use of hyperbole in relation to the use of outright lies. Are they the same? Different? Which one can be viewed in a comic light?

2. Discuss the crowd as they leave the courtroom. What are they in search of? Does this have anything to do with a desire for justice? In what ways can this be seen as a warning against the danger of crowds?

Chapter 4: Congratulatory
Chapter 5: The Jackal

Summary

Dr. Manette, Lucie, Lorry, and Stryver are congratulating Charles Darnay in a passageway outside the courtroom. Darnay kisses Lucie's hand. Dr. Manette gives Darnay a mysterious look of "distrust," "dislike," and even "fear." The group leaves the courthouse and encounters Sydney Carton. Lorry and Carton discuss business. Lorry says that he puts his bank ahead of himself; Carton says that he has no business whatsoever.

Carton and Darnay dine at a nearby inn. They drink a toast to Lucie. Carton gets drunk and calls himself "a disappointed drudge." He tells himself that he hates Darnay because in Darnay he sees what he could have been.

Carton meets with Stryver the next morning. We learn that Carton "boils down" Stryver's legal briefs, making them into compact documents that Stryver can understand. Carton complains some more about his life; he calls Lucie "a golden-haired doll," while it is clear that Stryver is very fond of Lucie. The final paragraph shows Carton as a man who has wasted his abilities and emotions, and who has resigned himself to having nothing.

Analysis

The unexplained way in which Dr. Manette looks at Darnay foreshadows a coming ominous plot twist. Lorry and Carton are contrasted in this chapter; Lorry is a successful man with talent and ambition, and thus a job, while Carton has talent, but no ambition or desire to have a "business." Victorian readers would expect an idle man who wastes his talents to be pathetic, and Dickens does not disappoint them. Darnay functions as a mirror of an alternate, more successful life that Carton feels he could have had. In saying that he hates Darnay, Carton is really saying that he hates what has happened to his life.

We also see in this chapter that all three men—Darnay, Stryver, and Carton—have all taken an interest in Lucie Manette. Carton's description of her as "a golden-haired doll" is quite accurate; he has revealed her for what she is—a plaything who relies on the men around her for strength.

Study Questions

1. What is happening at the beginning of Chapter 4?
2. How does Darnay greet Lucie?
3. How does Dr. Manette look at Darnay? What does this mean?
4. What does their conversation reveal as the difference between Lorry and Carton?
5. What happens while Carton and Darnay are dining?
6. Why does Carton say that he hates Darnay?
7. Why do Stryver and Carton meet?
8. What does Carton say about Lucie?
9. What else does Carton complain about?
10. What does the final paragraph say about Sydney Carton?

Answers

1. Dr. Manette, Lucie, Lorry, and Stryver are congratulating Darnay on his acquittal.
2. He greets Lucie by kissing her hand.
3. He look at Darnay with "distrust," "dislike," and "fear."
4. Lorry is a man of ambition who believes in "business," while Carton, even though he has ability, lacks the desire to do anything.
5. Carton gets drunk and calls himself "a disappointed drudge."
6. He says that he hates Darnay because Darnay reflects everything good that Carton could have been.

7. They meet because Carton does Stryver's legal paperwork.

8. Carton calls Lucie "a golden-haired doll."

9. Carton complains more about his life and that he is always behind everybody else.

10. It says that Carton has given up all hope of making anything of his life.

Suggested Essay Topics

1. Write an essay about Sydney Carton. Can his lack of ambition be explained from the evidence given? Do you, as a reader, feel any sympathy for him? Why or why not?

2. Discuss the idea that one character can shed light on our view of another character. What does the conversation between Carton and Lorry reveal about each man? Besides the physical resemblance, how does Darnay function as a mirror for Carton?

Chapter 6: Hundreds of People

Summary

It is four months later, and the trial is forgotten. Lorry is on his way to have Sunday dinner with the Manettes, whom he has befriended. The Manettes live in a quaint London house, where Dr. Manette receives his patients. Lorry arrives at the Manette house and talks with Miss Pross as he awaits the Manettes' return. He is surprised to see that Dr. Manette still has a bench and tools from his shoemaking days. Miss Pross tells Lorry that "hundreds of people" come to visit "Ladybird," her pet name for Lucie. She says that all of these people are unworthy of Lucie; Miss Pross believes that only her brother, Solomon, is worthy of Lucie—even though her brother has left Miss Pross in poverty by stealing everything that she possessed. Lorry admires miss Pross' unswerving devotion.

Lorry and the Manettes have dinner; Charles Darnay shows up, and Dr. Manette briefly gives him a strange look again. Sydney Carton drops by, but no "hundreds of people" turn up. The corner where the Manettes' house is located is said to possess a curious acoustical quality: the echoes of distant footsteps sound as if they are very close by. A storm approaches, and the echoes grow louder as people hurry to take shelter. The chapter ends with these lines: "Perhaps, see the great crowd of people with its rush and roar, bearing down upon them, too."

Analysis

This chapter can be seen as the calm before the storm. Lorry has betrayed his business sense by becoming friends with the Manettes, which is not a bad thing. There is a sense of normality and quietness to this chapter, but hints are given that this quiet normalcy is about to be shattered. The fact that Dr. Manette still has his shoemaking tools and bench shows that he cannot forget the horrors of his imprisonment. Dr. Manette again gives Darnay that mysterious look of distrust and dislike. The echoing footsteps are an obvious foreshadowing that something involving crowds of people is about to happen. And the coming storm can be seen as yet another symbol of trouble to come. The final paragraph of this chapter further shows that something ominous is bearing down on the people in Dr. Manette's house.

Study Questions

1. Where is Mr. Lorry going at the beginning of this chapter?

2. What is the tone of this chapter?

3. Is Miss Pross' claim that "hundreds of people" visit the house accurate?

4. What has Miss Pross' brother done to her?

5. What has Dr. Manette kept as a reminder of his 18 years in prison?

6. Who else comes to the Manettes' house on this Sunday?

7. What is odd about Dr. Manette's house?

8. Of what is this symbolic?

9. What happens when a storm approaches?

10. What is foreshadowed by the storm?

Answers

1. He is on his way to dine with Lucie and Dr. Manette, with whom he has become friends.

2. This chapter starts out with a tone of quiet normality but conveys an ominous sense that this normality is about to be shattered.

3. No. In fact, only three visitors show up on this day.

4. He has stolen everything that she owns, yet she still holds him in high esteem.

5. He has kept his shoemaker's bench and tools.

6. Charles Darnay and Sydney Carton are the other visitors.

7. The house has an acoustical property that allows distant footsteps to be heard as if they were up close.

8. These distant footsteps are symbolic of the danger that is coming to the people in the house.

9. The sound of echoing footsteps grows louder as people hurry for shelter from the storm.

10. The storm foreshadows that something ominous is about to happen.

Suggested Essay Topics

1. Write about foreshadowing in this chapter. Take into account the idea of "hundreds of people," the approaching storm, the echoing footsteps, and the final paragraphs. What do all of these things anticipate?

2. Discuss the symbolism of the shoemaker's bench. Why has Dr. Manette kept the bench? What does this say about him?

Chapter 7: Monseigneur in Town
Chapter 8: Monseigneur in the Country

New Characters:

Monsieur the Marquis: *French nobleman and Uncle of Charles Darnay*

A tall man in a nightcap: *the marquis' coach runs over and kills his child*

The mender of roads: *a French peasant*

Monsieur Gabelle: *servant of the Marquis*

Summary

The scene is a reception in Paris thrown by the Marquis. The scene is decadent; the Marquis has four people serving him chocolate. He is ironically called noble for thinking that "The earth and the fulness thereof are mine." The party is populated by ne'er-do-wells who have no saving grace, except that they are all "perfectly dressed." A storm comes, and the party breaks up.

The Marquis is described as a man of 60 with a "face like a fine mask," treacherous and cruel, yet "handsome." He departs for his chateau in the countryside; his carriage drives crazily through the streets until it hits something and the horses stop. The Marquis sees a tall man in a nightcap, holding a baby that has been killed by the carriage. The Marquis blames the accident on the peasants, whom he calls "you people," and wonders if his horses have been injured. Ernest Defarge emerges from the gathering crowd and tells the man that it is good his baby died quickly without pain; he questions if it "could have lived an hour so happily?" The Marquis throws a coin to Defarge and drives away. The coin comes flying back at the carriage. The Marquis continues on to his chateau, stopping only to talk to the mender of roads, who tells him that a man was riding along on the outside of the carriage. The Marquis tells Monsieur Gabelle to find this man.

Upon arrival at the chateau, the Marquis asks a servant, "Monsieur Charles, whom I expect; is he arrived from England?" His servant replies, "Monseigneur, not yet."

Analysis

These chapters show the decadence and callousness of the French nobility, a class that cares only about pleasure and about how they dress. The Marquis kills a child and is indifferent. The gap between the classes is so large that the Marquis does not even realize that Defarge is threatening the class structure by outwardly saying that the peasants would be better off dead; therefore, they have no fear of dying for a cause. The man riding on the outside of the Marquis' carriage foreshadows the coming struggle and the nobility's total ignorance of its coming. The Marquis asks his servant if Charles from England has arrived, leaving the reader to wonder as to *this* Charles' relationship to Charles Darnay.

Study Questions

1. What is the Marquis' party like?

2. What does the Marquis believe about himself?

3. Describe what the Marquis looks like.

4. What happens as the Marquis is traveling to his chateau?

5. What is his reaction to this?

6. What does Defarge say to the distraught man in the nightcap?

7. What does Defarge do with the coin that the Marquis throws to him?

8. What does the mender of roads tell the Marquis?

9. What does this man represent?

10. How does this chapter end?

Answers

1. It is incredibly decadent, full of morally corrupt people who are only concerned with how they look.

2. He believes that "the earth and the fulness thereof are mine."

3. He is 60 years old, with a cruel "face like a fine mask."

4. His carriage runs over and kills a small child.

5. He blames the peasants and is so indifferent that he cares more about his horses.

6. He tells the man that the child is better off dead because it would have been impossible for the child to have a happy life.

7. He throws the coin at the carriage as it is driving away.

8. He tells the Marquis that a man was riding on the outside of the carriage.

9. He represents the fact that the nobility has no idea that the peasants have any power.

10. The chapter ends with the Marquis awaiting the arrival of "Charles...from England."

Suggested Essay Topics

1. This chapter portrays the French nobility for the first time in the book. How are they portrayed? What is the effect of placing this directly after the ominous warning of the previous chapter?

2. Write an essay describing how the nobility have no awareness of what the peasants are capable of. Pay close attention to the accident and to what Defarge says and does, as well as to the man riding along with the carriage.

Chapter 9: The Gorgon's Head

Summary

The Marquis' chateau is said to be made of stone "as if the Gorgon's head had surveyed it." The Marquis sits down to dinner; he thinks he hears something outside, but a servant assures him that it is nothing. The Marquis' nephew finally arrives; he is indeed

Charles Darnay. Darnay and his uncle have a strained relationship. Darnay feels that the family name is detested all over France. His uncle replies, "Detestation of the high is the involuntary homage of the low." They continue to argue, with Darnay saying that the family has done "a world of wrong." The Marquis argues that class distinctions are necessary; he tells Darnay, "Better to be a rational creature...and accept your natural destiny." Darnay then renounces France and the property that will be his upon the death of his uncle; he tells the Marquis that he wants to settle in England. They retire for the evening.

In the morning, a crowd has gathered in the town; the news that the Marquis has been murdered has traveled fast. The Marquis is described as having been turned to stone, a knife through his heart. A note attached to the knife says: "Drive him fast to his tomb. This, from JACQUES."

Analysis

The stone look of the Marquis' chateau represents the hard, unfeeling nature of the nobility. The Marquis becomes briefly frightened when he thinks that someone is outside, but he quickly forgets, oblivious to the fact that he could be in any real danger.

The arrival of Charles Darnay begins to explain his secret trips between England and France although only a slight amount of information is revealed. This deepens the plot's mystery. Darnay and his uncle debate the whole class system. This allows Dickens to show how the ruling class felt that they were naturally superior to the peasants. Darnay's argument that his family has caused nothing but suffering seems a more reasonable way of looking at the situation.

The murder of the Marquis shows that the peasants can only take so much mistreatment before they violently revolt. Dickens shows how violence can easily lead to more violence: The Marquis kills a child and pays for it with his life.

Study Questions

1. What is the Marquis' chateau like?

2. What happens when the Marquis sits down to dinner?

3. What does this reveal about the Marquis?

4. Who is the nephew of the Marquis?

5. How does Darnay feel about the family name?

6. What does his uncle reply?

7. What is the larger issue at stake in this conversation?

8. What is the Marquis' final word about class?

9. What does Darnay do concerning the property in France?

10. How does this chapter end?

Answers

1. His chateau is described as silent and made of stone.

2. He thinks that he hears somebody outside but quickly forgets about it.

3. It reveals that he thinks he is protected from any harm because of his class.

4. Charles Darnay is the Marquis' nephew.

5. Darnay feels that the family name is feared and detested throughout France.

6. He tells Darnay: "Detestation of the high is the involuntary homage of the low."

7. Darnay and the Marquis are debating the whole idea of class structure.

8. He feels that it is "Better to be a rational creature...and accept your natural destiny."

9. He renounces the property, and he renounces France, deciding that he wants to settle in England for good.

10. The chapter ends with the Marquis murdered in his bed.

Suggested Essay Topics

1. Write an essay that provides an overview of the argument that Darnay and the Marquis have about class structure. Whose argument is more convincing? Why?

2. Describe the symbolism of stone in this chapter. How does the myth of the Gorgon relate to the scene? Keep in mind the description of the murdered Marquis as a "stone face" with a "stone figure" attached.

Chapter 10: Two Promises
Chapter 11: A Companion Picture

Summary

It is one year later. Charles Darnay is now a tutor of French and French Literature in England, as well as a translator. He has made a success of himself by finding a labor and dedicating himself to it. Darnay meets with Dr. Manette and reveals that he loves Lucie and wants to marry her. Darnay assures Dr. Manette that this marriage will strengthen the bond between father and daughter, a bond formed after 18 years of imprisonment. Dr. Manette tells Darnay that Lucie may have two other suitors, Mr. Stryver and Sydney Carton. Darnay informs Dr. Manette that he has a secret that he wished to share; Dr. Manette shouts "Stop!" and tells Darnay to wait until the morning of the wedding to reveal his secret. Darnay takes his leave.

Lucie returns home to find her father working at his shoe-maker's bench. She takes his hand and they walk up and down the hallway together for a long while.

Meanwhile, Mr. Stryver is informing Sydney Carton that he intends to marry Lucie. Stryver also tells Carton that he has no social skills, that he is "an insensible dog," and that he should find a wife who will take care of him, "against a rainy day." Carton replies, "I'll think about it."

Analysis

Darnay's occupation as a tutor of French refers to the idea that one needs an occupation to be considered a good person; it also shows that he has not completely forsaken his French past.

Dr. Manette's refusal to hear Darnay's secret until the morning of the wedding reveals that it must be a shocking secret indeed, something that Manette may already know, but may not yet be willing to face. Dr. Manette returns to his shoemaker's bench; this suggests that something has reminded him of his imprisonment. Dr. Manette will continue to return to the shoemaker's bench whenever he encounters something that reminds him of his lost 18 years. Lucie gently helps him regain his sense, just as she helped him regain his memory.

Stryver comes across as arrogant. He believes that Lucie will readily marry him, and he puts down Carton, despite the fact that Carton does all of Stryver's legal work. Stryver's remark that Carton should find a woman who will protect him "against a rainy day" shows who the real "insensible dog" is.

Study Questions

1. What is Charles Darnay's occupation?

2. What does this reveal about his character?

3. What do Darnay and Dr. Manette discuss?

4. How does Dr. Manette react when Darnay tells him that he has a secret to reveal to him?

5. What does Dr. Manette do after Darnay leaves?

6. What does this reveal about Dr. Manette's character?

7. How does Lucie help Dr. Manette when she finds him at the shoemaker's bench?

8. What does Stryver wish to confide to Carton?

9. What is Stryver's opinion of Carton?

10. Why is this opinion problematic?

Answers

1. He is a tutor of French language and literature.

2. This shows that he is industrious and that he has not forgotten his past in France.

3. They discuss Darnay's intention to marry Lucie.

4. He tells Darnay to wait until the morning of the wedding to reveal his secret.

5. He returns to making shoes.

6. It shows that he cannot forget his past, either; his way of dealing with this past is by returning to it.

7. She takes his hand and walks with him for a long while.

8. He tells Carton that he intends to marry Lucie.

9. Stryver has a low opinion of Carton, telling him that he lacks social grace and is "an insensible dog."

10. It reveals Stryver as a hypocrite since it is Carton who does all of Stryver's legal work.

Suggested Essay Topics

1. Write an essay comparing Darnay's revelation that he wants to marry Lucie to Stryver's revelation of the same intentions. Whom do the two men respectively tell? How do they speak of their desire? Who seems more likely to marry Lucie? Why?

2. Discuss Stryver's opinion of Carton. How is this ironic? Keep in mind what Carton does for Stryver. What can be made of Stryver's opinion that Carton should marry a woman who will protect him "against a rainy day"?

Chapter 12: The Fellow of Delicacy
Chapter 13: The Fellow of No Delicacy

Summary

Mr. Stryver decides to tell Lucie of his intentions, "to make her happiness known to her." He sees his desire to marry her in terms of a legal case that he has a good chance of winning. Stryver decides to stop into Tellson's Bank to tell Mr. Lorry of his intentions. Lorry exclaims "Oh dear me!" when told of Stryver's plan. As a businessman, Lorry says that he has no opinion on the matter; as a friend of the Manettes, he advises against it. He tells Stryver that "the young lady goes before all," that nothing else matters. Stryver says Lucie must be a "mincing fool" if she does not want to marry him. Stryver takes Lorry's advice to heart, proclaiming that he was uncertain of his intentions anyway. He proclaims that it is impossible to control the "vanities and giddinesses of empty-headed girls."

Sydney Carton pays Lucie Manette a visit. She sees that he looks ill and asks him if it is not "a pity to live no better life?" Carton declares that it is too late. Lucie becomes upset; Carton says, "God bless you for your sweet compassion." He tells her that he loves her, that she is too good for him, and that he would "give his life" for her. He asks her to keep this conversation in the strictest confidence and takes his leave.

Analysis

This chapter reveals Stryver as arrogant. He cannot admit to himself that a rational being would not want to marry him; Lucie Manette is a "mincing fool" if she will not have him. Lorry is capable of separating business from friendship, an ability which means that both can co-exist within him now.

Lucie is once again portrayed as full of compassion. No explanation is given as to why Carton loves her; it seems that every man who sees her falls in love with her. Yet all we know about Lucie is that she has a great store of "compassion." Carton's pledge that he would "give his life" for Lucie is something for the reader to keep in mind.

Study Questions

1. What does Stryver decide to do at the beginning of the chapter?

2. What is the gist of Stryver's conversation with Lorry?

3. How does Stryver react to this?

4. What does this say about his character?

5. Is Lorry capable of having both a business life and a personal life?

6. What is Stryver's final comment about Lucie?

7. Who pays a call on Lucie?

8. How does Carton look to Lucie?

9. What does Carton tell Lucie?

10. Why does Carton love Lucie?

Answers

1. He decides to tell Lucie of his intentions so that she may know she is going to be happy.

2. Lorry tells Stryver that he should not ask Lucie to marry him.

3. He proclaims that Lucie must be "a mincing fool" if she will not marry him.

4. It shows that he is very arrogant and bitter.

5. Yes, he finally is. He achieves this by making a clear distinction between business and friendship.

6. He says that "you cannot control...the giddinesses of empty-headed girls."

7. Sydney Carton pays a call of Lucie.

8. He looks ill and she asks what she can do to help him.

9. He tells her that he loves her and that he is willing to die for her.

10. From the evidence given, it must be because of her "sweet compassion."

Suggested Essay Topics

1. Discuss the character of Mr. Stryver in relation to his plan to marry Lucie. What do we learn about him as this plan falls apart? What do his comments about Lucie reveal about his personality?

2. Explore just what is meant by Lucie's "compassion." How does she relate to Sydney Carton? Why does he love her? What else do we know about Lucie, besides her capacity for compassion? Is her character meant to be a personification of just this one trait, or does this seem unintentional? Explain.

Chapter 14: The Honest Tradesman

Summary

Jerry Cruncher is sitting on his stool outside Tellson's Bank. A funeral procession passes by; it is the funeral of Roger Cly, Charles Darnay's former servant. There is a mob following the funeral vehicles, shouting "Spies! Pull'em out, there!" The narrator writes, "A crowd in those times stopped at nothing, and was a monster much dreaded." Jerry Cruncher joins the crowd as they proceed to the cemetery. The crowd becomes violent, proceeds to window-breaking, and then engages in looting, before breaking up. Cruncher and his son return home. His wife asks him if he is "going out to-night." Mr. Cruncher does go out late at night; he takes with him a sack, a crowbar, and some rope and chain. Young Jerry secretly follows him to the cemetery, where he sees his father digging up a grave. Young

Jerry runs home in horror. In the morning, Jerry and his wife argue about this "dreadful business." Young Jerry asks his father what a "resurrection-man" is. Mr. Cruncher replies that a resurrection-man" is an honest tradesman whose goods are "person's bodies."

Analysis

This chapter provides a bit of comedy. Jerry Cruncher calls himself "an honest tradesman," when in reality he is a grave-robber. This is a play on the idea that every man needs an occupation; Jerry knows this, but he sees nothing wrong in digging up bodies.

A violent crowd is presented in this chapter, with the narrator directly stating that crowds are dangerous. This is an ominous forewarning of even more violent mob action to come.

It is important to keep in mind the idea that all subplots will eventually tie into the main story; remember what Jerry Cruncher does at the cemetery, and remember whose funeral had been on that same day.

Study Questions

1. What passes by Tellson's Bank?
2. What is the crowd shouting?
3. What does the crowd do after the body is put in the ground?
4. Mr. Cruncher takes what tools with him when he goes out later that night?
5. Why does young Jerry follow his father? What does he find out?
6. What does Mrs. Cruncher think of her husband's "occupation"?
7. How does Mr. Cruncher view his "occupation"?
8. Why does young Jerry ask his father what a resurrection-man is?
9. What is comedic about this chapter?
10. Whose body could be inferred to have been dug up?

Answers

1. A funeral procession, followed by a large mob.

2. They are shouting "Spies! Pull 'em out!"

3. They proceed to go on a rampage of violence and looting until a rumor spreads that the guard is coming.

4. He takes a crowbar, a sack, and some rope and chain.

5. He is curious as to his father's "business." He finds his father digging up a grave.

6. She thinks it is a "dreadful business."

7. He calls himself "an honest tradesman."

8. It is young Jerry's way of letting his father know that he approves of the grave-robbing business.

9. Mr. Cruncher actually believes that grave-robbing is an honest trade; thus he fits the Victorian ideal of having a "labor."

10. We can infer that is the Roger Cly's body.

Suggested Essay Topics

1. Write an essay about Jerry Cruncher's "business." How does this compare with what Mr. Lorry has said about needing an occupation? What does it say about the class structure in England?

2. How does Jerry Cruncher relate to his family in this chapter? Compare this to events at the Manette household. What does this say about class structure in England?

Chapter 15: Knitting

Summary

The scene is the Defarges' wine-shop, where there has been much activity of late. Ernest Defarge brings the mender of roads to the wineshop and introduces him as "Jacques" to the other "Jacques." The mender of roads tells what he knows about the tall man in the nightcap: how he first saw him hanging on to the Marquis' carriage, how he next saw this man, with his arms bound to his sides, being taken somewhere by soldiers. The mender of roads says that he does not know what became of this prisoner. He has heard a rumor that a petition has been presented to the King explaining that the man was in great distress because the Marquis had callously killed his child. The mender of roads thinks that this petition may have saved the man's life. One of the Jacques tells him that a petition was presented to the King, by none other than Ernest Defarge. This petition was ignored, and the man was hanged on a 40-foot gallows that was erected in the town square.

The Jacques decide that the whole Evremonde family should be "registered," that is, their names are taken down as people to be executed when the revolution arrives. This register is what Madame Defarge is knitting; she knits the name, in code, of those who are to die. The Defarges take the mender of roads to see the King and Queen pass by in their coach. The mender of roads joins in the jubilation of seeing royalty; Defarge tells him that he is "a good boy" because "you make these fools believe that it will last forever. Then, they are the more insolent, and it is nearer ended."

Analysis

This chapter shows how the revolution is nearing, with the Defarges masterminding the insurrection in St. Antoine. Ernest Defarge brings the mender of roads into the fold, by telling him what happened to the man who killed the Marquis. The Defarges want to encourage people like the mender of roads to vocally support the King and Queen, since this will give the nobility a false sense of security, thus making them commit more callous acts, which in turn will lead to more insurrection. When they are watching the King and Queen pass, Madame Defarge tells the mender of roads that "if you were shown a great heap of dolls, and were set upon them to pluck them to pieces...for your own advantage, you would pick the richest and gayest...and if you were shown a flock of birds, unable to fly, and were set upon them to strip them of their feathers for your own advantage, you would set upon the birds of the finest feathers; would you not?" The mender of roads agrees; Madame Defarge tells him, "You have seen both dolls and birds to-day" and sends him off to think about this. These metaphors explain the Defarges' revolutionary ideas in terms that the peasants can easily understand.

Study Questions

1. Why does Defarge bring the mender of roads to the wine-shop?

2. Who presents the petition to the King and what was the result?

3. What does it mean to be "registered?"

4. How is this register kept secret?

5. Where do the Defarges take the mender of roads?

6. How does the mender of roads act?

7. Why is Ernest Defarge happy with the way the mender of roads acts?

8. What does Madame Defarge say about dolls and birds?

9. To whom is she referring?

10. How does this scene end?

Answers

1. He brings the mender of roads to the wine-shop, so that the mender of roads can hear the whole story of the man in the nightcap.

2. Ernest Defarge presented the petition to the King; it was ignored and the man was executed.

3. A person who is registered is marked to be killed when the revolution arrives.

4. Madame Defarge secretly knits the register in code.

5. They take him to see the King and Queen pass by.

6. He joins in the applause for the King and Queen.

7. He is happy because he feels that this adoration will lull the nobility into a false sense of security, thus allowing the revolution to begin sooner.

8. She tells the mender of roads that he would naturally attack the finest birds and dolls if it were to his advantage.

9. "Birds" and "dolls" represent the French ruling class.

10. Madame Defarge sends the mender of roads home to think about what she has told him.

Suggested Essay Topics

1. Explain how the Defarges are slowly building support for the revolution in this chapter. What thoughts do they plant in the head of the mender of roads? How do they do this in a subtle way? Pay attention to Madame Defarge's use of metaphor.

2. Write an essay about the mender of roads. Is there a difference between him and the Defarges? Does he seem aware that a revolution is brewing? Are the Defarges manipulating him for their own designs in the same way that the nobility has been? Why or why not?

Chapter 16: Still Knitting

Summary

The mood in St. Antoine has changed; it now bears a "cruel look of being avenged, which they would henceforth bear for ever." The Defarges make a trip to Paris to speak with "Jacques of the police." He informs them that there is a spy in their quarters: John Barsard, a "rather handsome" man whose nose has "a peculiar inclination towards the left cheek." The Defarges return to the wine-shop. Various Jacques are sitting around talking when a man enters the wine-shop. Madame Defarge puts a rose in her hat; the conversations break up, and the Jacques slowly disperse. This man speaks with Madame Defarge, asking her about her family, trying to get her to say something incriminating. This man fits the description of John Barsard; Madame Defarge knits his name as she speaks to him. Ernest Defarge comes in; Barsard asks him about Dr. Manette. He wonders if they have kept in touch. Defarge says no; Barsard informs him that Lucie is going to marry the nephew of the Marquis, Charles Darnay, in England. Barsard takes his leave.

Defarge tells his wife that he hopes the Manettes and Lucie stay out of France if the revolution ever comes. Madame Defarge reminds him that Darnay and his entire family are registered. The chapter ends with Madame Defarge and other women, "knitting, knitting, counting dropping heads."

Analysis

This chapter reveals that the Defarges have a serious organization of revolutionaries. They have friends in the police and secret signals that all of the Jacques know, such as the rose in the hat. Madame Defarge is shown to have no compassion; she knits

Barsard's name as she speaks with him, and her only response to her husband's wish that Darnay and the Manettes stay out of France is to remind him that they are all registered.

The plot thickens in this chapter. The revolution is quickly approaching; there are spies and counter-spies. Ernest Defarge begins an internal moral debate with himself about his loyalties, to Dr. Manette and to the cause of revolution. *A Tale of Two Cities* is building towards its climax.

Study Questions

1. Why do the Defarges go to Paris?

2. What do they learn there?

3. What is distinctive about John Barsard?

4. Why does Madame Defarge put a rose in her hat?

5. What is Madame Defarge doing while she speaks with Barsard?

6. What does Barsard tell the Defarges about the Manettes?

7. How does Ernest Defarge react to this?

8. What would happen if Darnay and the Manettes were to come to France?

9. How does Madame Defarge feel about this?

10. What are Madame Defarge and the other women doing as the chapter ends?

Answers

1. They go to Paris to meet with "Jacques of the police."

2. They learn that there is a spy in St. Antoine, by the name of John Barsard.

3. He has a crooked nose.

4. It is a signal to the Jacques that there is a suspicious stranger amongst them.

5. She is knitting his name, thus condemning him to death.

6. He tells them that Lucie Manette is going to marry the nephew of the Marquis.

7. He hopes that the Manettes stay in England.

8. They would be killed as nobility when the revolution arrived.

9. She is indifferent, saying only that they are registered.

10. They are "knitting, knitting, counting dropping heads."

Suggested Essay Topics

1. Write an essay about Madame Defarge. Is she portrayed as lacking compassion? Pay close attention to her interaction with John Barsard and to her reaction to the news about the Manettes. Contrast this with the compassionate character of Lucie Manette.

2. What does Ernest Defarge's reaction to the news about the Manettes reveal about him? How is he different from his wife in this respect? Between what are his loyalties split? How does this complicate matters for him?

Chapter 17: One Night
Chapter 18: Nine Days

Summary

It is the night before Lucie's wedding. She and her father are sitting in the moonlight, under the plane tree. They are both very happy as they assure each other that Lucie's marriage will not change their close relationship. Dr. Manette says to Lucie, "my future is far brighter, Lucie, seen through your marriage, than it could have been…without it." Dr. Manette speaks to Lucie of his imprisonment for the first time; he tells her that he thought often of his daughter who did not know he was alive. He says to her, "My thoughts, when they were wildest, never rose near the happiness that I have known with you." Lucie prays that night "that she may ever be as true to him as her love aspired to be, and as his sorrows deserved."

In the morning, Darnay tells Dr. Manette his secret. Mr. Lorry notices that Dr. Manette looks pale, a pallor which he takes as an

"indication that the old air of avoidance and dread had lately passed over him." The couple is married with only Mr. Lorry and Miss Pross in attendance. Mr. Lorry gushes over how beautiful Lucie is; he reflects on what his life might have been like if he had married 50 years ago. Dr. Manette tells Darnay, "Take her, Charles! She is yours!" They leave on their honeymoon. Lorry checks in at the bank; when he returns to the Manettes' house, Miss Pross informs him that Dr. Manette is "making shoes." Manette does not remember Lorry; Lorry realizes that it is useless to talk to him. This goes on for nine days.

Analysis

Light is shed on the closeness that bonds Lucie and her father. She feels that he deserves love because of his previous sorrow; he describes himself as being happier than he ever could have imagined. Yet the dark specter of Darnay's secret looms over this happiness. The reader still does not know what this secret is. It has something to do with Dr. Manette's imprisonment in France and with Darnay's past in France, but the connection is still mysterious and unclear. The extent to which this secret affects Dr. Manette is made clear when it prompts him to return to making shoes.

Lucie's compassion is once again illustrated through her prayer for her father. Dr. Manette telling Darnay, "Take her, Charles! She is yours!" once again illustrates that Lucie has no identity of her own; she is spoken of only in relation to the men in her life.

Study Questions

1. Of what do Lucie and her father assure each other on the night before her wedding?

2. What does Dr. Manette speak of for the first time?

3. What does Lucie pray for that night?

4. How does Dr. Manette react to hearing Darnay's secret?

5. Who is present at the wedding?

6. What does Dr. Manette say to Darnay after the wedding?

7. What does this reveal about Lucie's character?

8. What does Dr. Manette do after Lucie and Charles leave?

9. How does Lorry react to this? What does he try to do?

10. How long does this go on?

Answers

1. They assure each other that Lucie's marriage will only make them closer.

2. He speaks of his 18 years in prison.

3. She prays that she may be able to stay as devoted to her father as she now is.

4. He hides his distress well, but Lorry notices that something is wrong.

5. Besides Lucie, Charles, and Dr. Manette, only Lorry and Miss Pross are at the wedding.

6. He says, "Take her, Charles! She is yours!"

7. It reveals that her character is defined according to her relationship to the men around her.

8. He returns to "making shoes."

9. He tries to talk to Dr. Manette, but soon realizes that it is useless. He can do nothing except keep watch over Dr. Manette.

10. It goes on for nine days.

Suggested Essay Topics

1. How does Dr. Manette react to the marriage of his daughter? What does he say to Darnay? Does it seem that it is something other than his daughter's marriage that has led him back to his shoemaker's bench?

2. Explore what we know about Charles Darnay's secret. Think of his past as well as Dr. Manette's past. Keep in mind Dr. Manette's reaction upon learning the secret. Why do we still not know the whole secret? Examine how the clues to the nature of the secret are revealed.

Chapter 19: An Opinion
Chapter 20: A Plea

Summary

On the morning of the tenth day, Dr. Manette has regained his senses. Mr. Lorry decides not to confront Dr. Manette directly about his problem; he speaks to Manette of "a curious case in which I am deeply interested." Dr. Manette has no recall of the past nine days. He tells Lorry that "the relapse was not unforeseen by its subject." He tells Lorry that the "subject" is greatly burdened, yet unable to speak about this burden. Manette assures Lorry that the worst is over. Lorry convinces Manette that the shoemaker's bench should be destroyed; he couches this discussion by speaking of a man returning to a forge to do blacksmith work. Manette tells Lorry to destroy it in the name of his daughter. Two weeks later, Dr. Manette goes to join Lucie and her husband; while he is gone, Lorry and Pross destroy the bench.

The honeymooners return to the house; Sydney Carton visits them. He talks with Manette about the dinner they had together in the past. Carton asks Darnay to forgive him for being rude; Darnay says he has not thought about it. He thanks Carton again for helping to have him acquitted all those years ago. Later that night, Lucie asks Charles to be "very lenient with Carton," and to "believe that he has a heart he...seldom reveals, and that there are deep wounds on it." She tells him, "I have seen it bleeding." The narrator says that if Carton had heard this exchange, he would have once more proclaimed, "God bless her for her sweet compassion!"

Analysis

Once again, Lorry uses his business sense to make a difficult situation easier. Just as he told Lucie that her father was alive by pretending that he was talking of somebody else, he talks to Dr. Manette about his situation by addressing the problem as if it were happening to someone other than Manette. His business acumen can be applied to his friendships. The smashing of the forge is symbolic of Manette letting go of the past. Sydney Carton's discussion with Darnay serves the same purpose although to a lesser degree. He clears the air with Darnay so that past worries can be put to rest. The chapter concludes with Dickens once again reminding us of Lucie's incredible compassion.

Study Questions

1. What happens after Dr. Manette's ninth day of making shoes?
2. How does Lorry approach Dr. Manette concerning his relapse?
3. What does Dr. Manette say about the cause of this relapse?
4. How does Lorry convince Manette to allow him to destroy the bench?
5. What is the symbolic nature of smashing the bench?
6. Who visits the couple upon their return from their honeymoon?

7. What do Carton and Darnay talk about?

8. What function does this serve?

9. What does Lucie ask her husband to do?

10. Why does she ask this of him?

Answers

1. He regains his composure and stops making shoes.

2. He tells Manette he wants to speak of "a curious case" that he knows of.

3. He says it is caused by an apprehension that the "subject" is unable to talk about.

4. He tells Manette that it should be done "for his daughter's sake."

5. It is symbolic of Dr. Manette's attempt to put the past behind him.

6. Sydney Carton is their first visitor.

7. Carton and Darnay speak of the trial and the meal they shared afterwards.

8. It serves to clear the air concerning past events.

9. She asks him to be generous and kind to Carton and to not speak ill of him when he is not present.

10. She says that she is aware of some deep wounds in Carton's soul that he keeps hidden from everybody else.

Suggested Essay Topics

1. Write an essay about Lorry's non-confrontational way of talking to Dr. Manette. Why does he employ this method? Has he used this method before? When? Why? How does this relate to his business sense?

2. How is the past put to rest in this chapter? Think of both Dr. Manette and Sydney Carton. What do they respectively do to come to terms with past events? Do they both seem to meet with success? Why or why not?

Chapter 21: Echoing Footsteps

New Character:

Little Lucie: *daughter of Charles and Lucie*

Summary

Time passes. Lucie hears the echoes of distant footsteps. On occasion this seems ominous, but for the most part she hears "in the echoes of years none but friendly and soothing sounds." She has one child, a daughter named Lucie. She has a boy child who

dies but even this is not a terribly sad occasion, as "the rustling of an Angel's wings got blended with the other echoes."

Six years pass, and various changes take place in the lives of the characters, but nothing shocking happens. Then, one night Mr. Lorry comes over. There is a storm; he tells them that "there is such an uneasiness in Paris, that we have actually had a run of confidence upon us!" He is calmed when he sees that everything is as usual at the Manette household.

The scene is not nearly so calm in St. Antoine; the peasants have taken up weapons and are led by the Defarges, storming the Bastille. Madame Defarge is heard shouting, "To me, women…we can kill as well as the men when the place is taken." Prisoners are freed; Defarge forces a guard to show him "One Hundred and Five North Tower." It is the cell where Dr. Manette had been held.

Defarge finds the initials A.M. carved into the wall, along with the words "a poor physician." The governor is killed, Madame Defarge cuts off his head, and heads are carried on spikes. The chapter ends with the hope that these footsteps stay out of Lucie Manette's life since "they are head long, mad and dangerous…(and) not easily purified when once stained red."

Analysis

Lucie's life is described as passing along uneventfully. The death of her child shows that she can withstand pain and suffering; this death also shows that tragedy is never very far away. The wish at the end of the chapter that the footsteps stay out of Lucie's life seems to say that this is impossible. The echoing footsteps that Lucie hears are indeed the distant footsteps in France.

The revolution finally begins; the power of crowds is finally unleashed in its full force. In the midst of this, Ernest Defarge takes the time to find out what "One Hundred and Five North Tower" is. The fact that he does this in the midst of chaotic violence is a testament to how much Dr. Manette is on his mind, perhaps even suggesting that Dr. Manette's imprisonment helped spark the revolutionary fervor within Defarge. Madame Defarge is described as a brutal woman who takes easily to murder. The final paragraph of the chapter refers to the wine that was spilled in the street many years earlier, but the wine is now truly blood; there is no way out of the violence of revolution once it has started.

Study Questions

1. How many children does Lucie have? What are their fates?

2. What does the death of the second child signify?

3. What else happens as six years pass?

4. What news does Mr. Lorry bring that marks the beginning of the end of normalcy?

5. What happens in Paris?

6. What does Ernest Defarge do in the midst of the storming of the Bastille?

7. Why is this important?

8. What does Madame Defarge do to the governor's dead body?

9. What does the final paragraph of this chapter have to say about Lucie?

10. To what event does the final paragraph refer?

Answers

1. She has two children. The daughter lives and flourishes while her son dies at a young age.

2. His death shows that tragedy is always close by.

3. The six years pass calmly, and Lucie and her family build a quiet, uneventful domestic life.

4. Lorry tells them that there has been a run of confidence on Tellson's because of the instability in France.

5. The peasants storm the Bastille.

6. He makes a guard take him to "One Hundred and Five, North Tower."

7. It reveals that Dr. Manette's imprisonment has deeply affected him.

8. She cuts off his head.

9. It states a hope that the events in France do not affect her quiet life in England.

10. It refers to the wine that was spilled in St. Antoine many years ago.

Suggested Essay Topics

1. How is Lucie's life described? Think of her two children and the mention of the echoing footsteps, as well as the hope in the final paragraph that events in France will not affect her. Even though Lucie is the focus of part of this chapter, is she described as doing anything? What is the significance of this?

2. Compare Madame Defarge to Lucie. Does Madame Defarge have compassion? What does she say about women and killing? What does she do to the governor's body? What do these things reveal about her? What emotions do Madame Defarge represent? Is she the opposite of the docile, passive Lucie?

Chapter 22: The Sea Still Rises
Chapter 23: Fire Rises

New Characters:

The Vengeance: *follower of Madame Defarge who participates in the revolt in France*

Foulon: *a French nobleman killed during the revolution*

Summary

One week has passed. Madame Defarge and one of her "sisterhood" are knitting. This woman has "already earned the complimentary name of The Vengeance." Ernest Defarge comes into the wine-shop, shouting that "old Foulon, who told the famished people they might eat grass," has been captured.

A crowd gathers to go to Foulon and serve him justice. Madame Defarge and The Vengeance go from house to house, "rousing the women." The women are described as leaving their children and the aged and sick to fend for themselves while they go out in "madness."

The crowd reaches Foulon; grass is stuffed into his mouth, and he is hanged from a lamppost. Madame Defarge is said to have treated him "as a cat might have done with a mouse." Word spreads that Foulon's son-in-law is on his way to Paris under a guard 500 strong. Yet the mob captures him and puts his head on a pike next to Foulon's.

The French countryside is described as ruined. The peasants burn down the Marquis' chateau. Monsieur Gabelle flees the chateau on horseback; no one is willing to help him extinguish the fire. The mob spares Gabelle's life, but "there were other functionaries less fortunate, that night...whom the rising sun found hanging across once-peaceful streets." The narrator states that there were also revolutionaries who were losing their lives as well.

Analysis

The sheer power of the crowd is further revealed in these chapters. Women are active, but they are full of "madness" and bloodlust as they seek "Vengeance." This representation of women serves to justify the passivity of Lucie as heroic. There seems to be no middle ground for women; either they are passive and full of "compassion" or active and searching for "Vengeance." Madame Defarge is especially evil, in the view of the narrator, as she plays a "cat and mouse game" with the dying Foulon. Vengeance is a frightening thing; the treatment of Foulon is horrifying. Yet he showed no concern for the starving peasants; no one is free of guilt in this chapter.

The killing of Foulon's son-in-law shows to what extent the peasants will go in their desire to be rid of the upper class. This can also be seen as foreshadowing what might happen, if, perhaps, the Marquis' nephew made his way to France. Chapter 23 ends, noting that death is occurring all over France, on both sides of the revolution.

Study Questions

1. How does Chapter 22 open?

2. What does Ernest Defarge tell the crowd at the wine-shop?

3. What is the result of this news?

4. How are the women who join Madame Defarge described?

5. What has Foulon said to the peasants before?

6. What is his fate?

7. Who joins him in this fate?

8. How could this relate to Charles Darnay?

9. How does Madame Defarge react towards Foulon?

10. What do the peasants do next?

Answers

1. Madame Defarge and The Vengeance are sitting in the wine-shop, knitting.

2. He tells them that Foulon has been captured.

3. A mob forms and proceeds to where Foulon is being imprisoned.

4. They are described as "mad" women who leave their children behind.

5. He has said of the starving peasants that they might eat grass.

6. His head winds up on a pike, with his mouth full of grass.

7. His son-in-law soon has his head on a pike, next to him.

8. It shows what may happen to Darnay, nephew of the Marquis, if he were to come to France.

9. She slowly kills him "as a cat might have done to a mouse."

10. They burn down the Marquis' chateau.

Suggested Essay Topics

1. Write an essay about how women are depicted in this chapter. Why are they described as mad? What does The Vengeance's name reveal? What about Madame Defarge's treatment of Foulon? Contrast these portrayals with Lucie's inactivity.

2. Is Dickens siding with the peasants or the nobility? Or is he treating both sides equally? Refer to what the peasants do, keeping in mind what the nobility has said and done.

Chapter 24: Drawn to the Loadstone Rock

Summary

Three years have passed. Royalty and the court are gone from France. Mr. Lorry decides to go to France to help at the unsettled Paris branch of Tellson's Bank. Darnay says that he wishes he was going to France. Lorry leaves, taking only Jerry Cruncher with him. The French ruling class has become exiled in England, planning how to get the country back. Charles Darnay is uneasy. Stryver suggests that the whole peasant class in France should be wiped out. It is revealed that only Dr. Manette knows Darnay's true connection to France. He secretly gets a letter addressed to the Marquis' nephew. It is a letter from Gabelle. Gabelle is now in prison because he has "acted for an emigrant," Darnay. Darnay sees the nobility being driven from France; he reasons that he has never oppressed anyone, so France must be safe for him. He resolves to go to France to save Gabelle. Darnay decides to leave in secret, making himself known to Lorry only upon arrival in Paris. Darnay begins his journey "as he left all that was dear on earth behind him." Thus ends the second section of the novel.

Analysis

This chapter sets up the action that will take place in the third and final section of *A Tale of Two Cities*. Lorry is off to France with Jerry Cruncher in tow. Charles Darnay decides to go to Paris, as well. One can guess what may happen next, recalling the treatment of Foulon's son-in-law. Darnay's decision to go to France seems completely unbelievable. He is aware of the peasants' attitude toward nobility, and his assurance that he will be safe because he renounced his own family name does not appear to be a convincing argument. Dickens' audience probably forgave him this heavy-handed plot device though. Darnay has to have some reason to go to France if the events of the final section are going to unfold. The warning that Darnay has "left all that was dear on earth behind him" hints that it will be difficult for him to reacquire what he has left behind.

Study Questions

1. How many years have passed between chapters?
2. Why does Lorry decide to go to France?
3. Whom does he take with him?
4. What has happened to the French nobility?
5. What is Mr. Stryver's opinion of the situation in France?
6. From whom does Charles Darnay receive a letter?
7. What decision does this letter lead Darnay to make?
8. Whom does he tell of his plans?
9. Why is this decision unbelievable?
10. What is the main function of this chapter?

Answers

1. Three years have passed.
2. He is going to help out at the chaotic Paris branch of Tellson's Bank.
3. He takes only Jerry Cruncher with him.
4. They are exiled in England, planning how to get their country back.
5. He thinks that the peasants should all be killed.
6. He receives a letter from Gabelle, the Marquis' functionary in France. Gabelle is now in prison.
7. Darnay decides to go to France to help Gabelle.
8. He keeps his plan secret, telling no one.
9. Darnay would have to be aware of the incredible danger he was putting himself in.
10. It serves to set up the action that will unfold in the novel's final section.

Suggested Essay Topics

1. Reflect on Darnay's decision to go to France. Does it seem

believable? Why is he going? Would he be aware of the danger he was placing himself in? Where do his loyalties lie?

2. Write an essay explaining how the action seems to be shifting towards France. Who goes to France? Can the rest of the plot be inferred from the information given so far? Are there any unresolved mysteries to hold reader interest?

Book the Third: The Track of a Storm

Chapter 1: In Secret

New Characters:

Various French patriot-citizens: *members of the peasant class who are now in power*

Summary

Charles Darnay meets difficulty on his way to Paris. He is stopped in every small town that he passes through and forced to show his papers before he can proceed. He quickly realizes that he cannot go back "until he should have been declared a good citizen at Paris."

In one small town, it is decided that Darnay will be provided an armed escort to Paris. Darnay notices that all the citizens are wearing red caps. He reaches Beauvais: he is called "a cursed emigrant" and "a cursed aristocrat." His claim that he has returned on his own accord falls on deaf ears.

Darnay hears one of the armed guards say that he will be "judged" at Paris. Darnay learns that a decree was just passed that takes all property rights away from emigrants; he learns that another decree is about to be passed, declaring that all emigrants be put to death. Darnay reaches France, where he is referred to as a "prisoner."

He is called Evremonde and sentenced to La Force prison. He objects but is told that emigrants have no rights. The officer writes "In secret" on a piece of paper and hands it to a guard. This guard happens to be Ernest Defarge. He asks Darnay if he is married to Dr. Manette's daughter. Darnay asks Defarge if he will help him; Defarge replies, "I will do nothing for you. My duty is to my country and my people."

Darnay learns that the King is in prison. Darnay, identified as Evremonde, is thrown in a cell; a fellow prisoner hopes Darnay is not "in secret." Darnay says that he does not understand what this means, but he has heard the guard say it of him. The chapter ends with Darnay thinking "He made shoes, he made shoes, he made shoes."

Analysis

This chapter reveals the fateful mistake that Charles Darnay has made: a mistake that leads him to prison. The revolution is gathering steam, and Darnay is caught in the middle of it. New decrees have been passed since he set out from England, decrees that doom him. The fact that he has renounced his property and his family means little to the patriots. His petition falls on deaf ears just as the peasants have always been ignored by the nobility. Dickens is showing that the nobility and peasants have traded places, with the peasants acting just as callously as the nobility has in the past.

We see that Defarge has decided that his allegiances lie with the revolutionary cause and not with personal relationships. The revolution has gathered so much steam that it is impossible for it to be stopped by personal considerations. Darnay finds out that he is "in secret." We do not know what this means, but it is a very ominous and suspenseful phrase. Darnay thinks of Dr. Manette upon his imprisonment and is able to grasp why Manette made shoes.

Study Questions

1. What difficulties does Darnay meet at the beginning of his journey?

2. How does he finally reach Paris?

3. What decrees have been passed since Darnay has left England?

4. How is Darnay referred to by the officer in Paris?

5. Whom does Darnay meet in Paris?

6. What does Ernest Defarge say to Darnay?

7. What ominous phrase is connected with Darnay's imprisonment?

8. What does Darnay learn of the King's fate?

9. What does Darnay think of when in his cell?

10. What is this a reference to?

Answers

1. He is stopped innumerable times and forced to show his papers before he can proceed.

2. He reaches Paris under an armed escort.

3. Emigrants have lost all of their property rights and may be condemned to death.

4. He is referred to as "the prisoner."

5. He meets Ernest Defarge.

6. He tells Darnay that he cannot help him because his allegiance is to the newly formed state.

7. The phrase is "in secret."

8. He learns that the King has been imprisoned.

9. He thinks, "He made shoes, he made shoes, he made shoes."

10. This is a reference to Dr. Manette's long imprisonment.

Suggested Essay Topics

1. Write an essay about how the Revolution is gaining momentum. What has happened since Darnay left England? What does Defarge's refusal to help Darnay say about the strength of the Revolution?

2. Compare the behavior of the empowered peasants to the behavior of the previous ruling class. How do they deal with personal appeals? Remember the Marquis and think of the treatment of Darnay's arguments.

Chapter 2: The Grindstone
Chapter 3: The Shadow

Summary

Tellson's Bank in France is in the house of a member of the nobility. The house has been seized by the newly formed republic and marked by the tricolor flag. There is a grindstone within the gates of the house. Mr. Lorry says, "Thank God that no one near and dear to me is in this dreadful town tonight."

Just as he says this, Dr. Manette and Lucie show up. They tell him that Charles is in a prison in Paris. A crowd of 40 to 50 people pours into the courtyard; they sharpen their various weapons at the grindstone. This crowd is described as blood-stained "savages."

Dr. Manette decides that, as a former prisoner in the Bastille, he has influence with these people. They lead him towards Paris, shouting, "Help for the Bastille prisoner's kindred in La Force." Mr. Lorry worries about compromising the bank by harboring the wife of an emigrant. He finds other lodgings for Lucie, her daughter, and Miss Pross.

Defarge comes to the bank with a note from Dr. Manette. The note says: "Charles is safe, but I cannot safely leave this place yet." Lorry, Defarge, and his wife take this note to Lucie, along with a note from Charles. Madame Defarge accompanies them so that "she may be able to recognize their faces...for their safety."

Madame Defarge is knitting. Lucie begs Madame Defarge to be merciful to her husband. Madame Defarge coldly replies that since she has seen so much suffering, "is it likely that the trouble of one wife and mother would be much to us now?" Lucie says, "That dreadful woman seems to have thrown a shadow on me and on all my hopes." Lorry tries to reassure Lucie, but "in his secret mind," he is "troubled greatly."

Analysis

This chapter brings all of the principal characters to France, just as Lorry ironically said that he was glad he had no loved ones here. Dr. Manette tries to put his imprisonment to good use, using it to show sympathy with the new republic, in hopes of freeing Darnay. Lorry has not abandoned his business sense; he removes Lucie from Tellson's in fear of compromising the bank.

It seems that Ernest Defarge may still have some loyalty to Dr. Manette since he is delivering the note to Lucie. Or, this may be a ploy so that Madame Defarge may see Darnay's family. She is knitting; one could assume that Lucie and her daughter are being registered. Madame Defarge dismisses Lucie's pleas on the grounds that the suffering of one person has no importance. Lucie does not

realize the extent to which she is in danger; the chapter ends with
Lorry starting to understand that Darnay and all his relations are
in great danger.

Study Questions

1. Where is Tellson's Paris branch located?
2. What is on the grounds of this house?
3. Who comes to France in this chapter?
4. What does Defarge bring to Mr. Lorry?
5. Where does Lorry take the Defarges?
6. Why does Madame Defarge accompany them?
7. Is this the only reason?
8. What does Lucie ask of Madame Defarge?
9. What does Madame Defarge reply?
10. What is Mr. Lorry thinking as the chapter ends?

Answers

1. It is located in a house that the republic has seized from a
   nobleman.
2. There is a grindstone on the grounds of the house.
3. Lucie, her daughter, Dr. Manette, and Miss Pross come to
   France.
4. He brings a note from Dr. Manette.
5. He takes them to see Lucie.
6. The reason given is that she may see them, so that they may
   be protected.
7. There are hints that Madame Defarge has another reason;
   she wants to see Lucie and the child so that she may register
   them.
8. She asks for her mercy concerning her husband.
9. She tells Lucie that one person's suffering has become irrel-
   evant.

10. He is greatly troubled as to Charles and Lucie's future.

Suggested Essay Topics

1. Describe Mr. Lorry's allegiances in this chapter. Does he put Lucie in danger by placing her in a less secure apartment? Does he seem to care more for the bank than for Lucie? Why or why not?

2. Explore the parallels between Lorry's allegiance to the bank and Ernest Defarge's allegiance to the republic. What are Defarge's allegiances? Can we be sure of them yet? How do personal considerations fit into both situations?

Chapter 4: Calm in Storm
Chapter 5: The Wood-Sawyer

Summary

Dr. Manette returns four days later; he assures Lucie that Charles was not killed during the violent attack against the prisoners. He does not tell Lucie that 1,100 other prisoners were not so lucky. Dr. Manette uses his status as "a notable sufferer under the overthrown system" to enter a plea before "the lawless court" to free Charles Darnay. While the court refuses to free Darnay, they allow Dr. Manette to stay around the prison to assure that Darnay is safe. Soon, using his influence, Dr. Manette becomes the inspecting physician in La Force. He sees Darnay on a regular basis, an arrangement which comforts Lucie.

The new republic begins under the banner of "Liberty, Equality, Fraternity, or Death." Beheadings are rampant, thanks to the invention of the guillotine, which is referred to as a "sharp female." One year and three months pass in this manner. Dr. Manette becomes known as the "Bastille Captive," a status that keeps him above all suspicions and questions.

Lucie remains true to Darnay through this time "as all the quietly loyal and good will always be." Her father takes her to a place where Darnay, looking out from his prison window, can sometimes see her. Lucie stands on this spot for two hours every day. This spot happens to be near the shop of a wood-sawyer (who happens to be the former mender of roads). He takes an interest in Lucie's activity, but declares, "It's not my business." One day Madame Defarge passes by this spot "like a shadow." The chapter ends with Dr. Manette telling Lucie and Lorry that "Charles is summoned for tomorrow."

Analysis

Dr. Manette begins to view his imprisonment in a new light; he is a hero to the new republic because of it, and he revels in this influence as he tries to get Charles Darnay free. The court of the new republic is presented as just as corrupt as the English Court that first tried Darnay and no better than the French court that it has replaced.

Lucie is once again shown as displaying a strong, quiet, passive resolve, this time in opposition to the deathly feminine guillotine. That fact that the spot where Lucie stands is outside the shop of the former mender of roads is another example of Dickens' reliance on melodramatic coincidence. The wood-sawyer's insistence, "It's not my business," followed presently by the appearance of Madame Defarge at this very spot, suggests that maybe he made it his business. Remember that he knows and supports the Defarges; this does not bode well for Lucie.

Study Questions

1. What does Dr. Manette keep secret from Lucie?

2. How does Dr. Manette gain influence with the new republic?

3. What is the slogan of this new republic?

4. What new device has led to more beheadings and how is this device described?

5. How does Lucie cope with her husband's imprisonment?

6. What small consolation does Dr. Manette arrange for Lucie and Charles?

7. Where is the coincidental location of this spot?

8. What interest does the wood-sawyer take in Lucie?

9. Yet, who passes by this very spot soon after?

10. How does this chapter end?

Answers

1. He does not tell her that 1,100 prisoners have been killed in the past four days.

2. He takes advantage of his status as a martyr in the eyes of the new republic.

3. "Liberty, Equality, Fraternity, or Death."

4. The guillotine is the device, and it is described as a "sharp female."

5. She displays her "quietly loyal...and good" strength.

6. He arranges for Lucie to stand on a spot where Charles can see her from his prison window.

7. It is right outside the shop of the wood-sawyer, who used to be the mender of roads.

8. He outwardly claims that what she is doing is none of his business.

9. Madame Defarge appears at this spot.

10. It ends with Dr. Manette announcing that Charles' trial will be on the next day.

Suggested Essay Topics

1. Write an essay about the change that takes place in Dr. Manette in this chapter. How is he using his imprisonment to his advantage? What change does this present in him? Why does his new position allow him to gain strength? How is this related to Darnay's suffering?

2. Discuss Lucie's behavior in this chapter. What activity does she undertake? How is her character development consistent with what has been said about her and with what she has said and done in earlier chapters?

Chapter 6: Triumph
Chapter 7: A Knock at the Door

Summary

Charles Darnay is called before the new republic's court: "a dread Tribunal of five judges, public prosecutor, and determined jury." The court is described in less-than-glowing terms; it looks as if "the felons were trying the honest men."

The trial begins; Darnay proceeds to present his case as Dr. Manette has directed. He tells the court that he is the son-in-law of Dr. Manette and that he has come back to France, voluntarily, to save a citizen's life. He addresses the crowd that has gathered: "Was that criminal in the eyes of the republic?" He is met with a resounding "No!"

Darnay is acquitted, and the crowd carries him home on their shoulders. When Lucie sees him, she drops "insensible in his arms."

Lucie says a prayer, and then Charles says of Dr. Manette, "No other man in all this France could have done what he has done for me."

This happiness is short-lived. Miss Pross and Jerry Cruncher go out shopping for food and wine. In the short time while they are gone, soldiers show up at Lucie and Charles' apartment. They arrest Darnay again, telling him that he has been "denounced—and gravely, by the Citizen and Citizeness Defarge." One other person has denounced Darnay, but the guards will not reveal this name, saying, "you will be answered to-morrow."

Analysis

This chapter once again illuminates the fickle nature of crowds and the danger of unpredictability that accompanies this fickleness. Darnay is playing to the sympathy of the crowd, as he was coached by Dr. Manette. His behavior in this chapter is reminiscent of the manner adopted by the attorney-general who tried to have Darnay convicted in England by playing on the jury's emotions. This shows that both systems of justice are corrupt, suggesting that the violent revolution will replace one unjust form of government with another.

Lucie's reaction upon seeing Charles is in character with her celebrated weakness. She collapses into his arms, physically overcome by emotion; still, she recovers quickly enough to offer a prayer. Her behavior exemplifies the Victorian ideal of the passive, emotional, worshipful woman; once again Lucie can be seen as the polar opposite of the active, violent, unfeeling Madame Defarge.

The earlier hints that the Defarges were up to something horrid begin to see their fruition here. They have conspired to denounce Darnay just at the moment when he is in high favor with the people and is happy and confident. In other words, he is blind to any vulnerability. His false sense of security makes it that much easier to hurt him; this follows the same philosophy that had the Defarges encouraging the mender of roads to cheer for the King and Queen. Finally, the mysterious nature of the accuser piques interest for the next chapter.

Study Questions

1. How is the court that tries Darnay described?

2. How does Darnay defend himself?

3. From whom did he learn to appeal to the court in this way?

4. What is the result of the trial?

5. To what can this courtroom scene be compared?

6. How does Lucie react upon seeing Charles?

7. What does Lucie do next?

8. What happens when Charles and Lucie return to their apartment?

9. How has this happened?

10. What mystery does the chapter end on?

Answers

1. It is a horrid place that looks as if "the felons were trying the honest men."

2. He reminds the court that he is the son-in-law of Dr. Manette and he appeals directly to the crowd's emotions.

3. Dr. Manette advised him to proceed in this way.

4. Darnay is acquitted.

5. It can easily be compared to Darnay's earlier trial in England.

6. She collapses "insensible" into his arms.

7. She recovers and offers a prayer to God.

8. Four soldiers show up and arrest Charles again.

9. The Defarges have denounced him.

10. It ends by saying that there is a third person who has denounced Darnay, but it does not reveal who this third person is.

Suggested Essay Topics

1. Write an essay comparing this trial with Darnay's earlier trial in England. Are the results the same? Pay attention to how these results were achieved. Notice any similarities in the way Darnay was prosecuted in England and the way he defends himself here. What does this say about systems of justice?

2. Describe the use of surprise and suspense in this chapter. Why is Darnay arrested again right after he is freed? How does this play on reader expectations? How does this relate to the Defarges' strategy of keeping the nobility unaware of the danger they are in?

Chapter 8: A Hand at Cards

Summary

Miss Pross and Jerry Cruncher, unaware of Darnay's arrest, continue to shop for dinner and wine. They enter a wine-shop; Miss

Pross is shocked to be standing face to face with her brother, Solomon. He tells her not to call him Solomon and quickly leads her outside. Solomon tells Miss Pross that he is now an official and very busy because of it. Cruncher interrupts the conversation to ask Solomon what his name was "over the water," in England, when he was "a spy-witness at the Bailey."

Before Solomon can answer, another voice says that Solomon's name was "Barsad." This voice belongs to Sydney Carton, who has just arrived in England, and has business he wishes to conduct with Barsad. Carton informs Miss Pross that her brother is a spy; he then "asks" Mr. Barsad to accompany him to Tellson's Bank to discuss some business.

Jerry Cruncher accompanies Carton and Barsad to the bank, where they inform Mr. Lorry that Charles Darnay has been arrested again. Carton states that "this is a desperate time, when desperate games are played for desperate stakes. Let the Doctor play the winning game; I will play the losing one…Any one carried home by the people to-day may be condemned to-morrow."

Carton then proceeds as if he is playing cards, with Barsad being the prize. Carton speaks of many reasons why the republic may find Barsad suspicious; he then plays his "ace," "denunciation of Mr. Barsad to the nearest section committee." Carton then finds that he has another card. Carton has seen Barsad with another suspicious man, Roger Cly. Barsad claims that Cly is dead; he even has the death certificate to prove it. Jerry Cruncher, upon hearing this, states, "you buried paving stones and earth in that there coffin."

Barsad admits that Cly's death was faked so that he could escape the angry mob in England; he is incredulous as to how Cruncher knows this. Carton finds out that Barsad can come and go as he pleases at the prison where Darnay is being held; Barsad tells Carton that it would be impossible to arrange an escape. Carton then insists that the final part of the bargain be conducted in secret, known only to himself and Barsad.

Analysis

This chapter overflows with plot. In another one of Dickens' famous coincidences, Barsad/Pross, Miss Pross, Jerry Cruncher, and Sydney Carton all meet on a street in St. Antoine. Carton's statement about playing the losing hand suggests that he has some plan to free Darnay that might endanger his own life. Jerry Cruncher is aware of what was buried in Cly's coffin; this refers back to Jerry's work as "an honest tradesman," or grave-robber. This coincidence verges on the unbelievable.

Carton's plan is not revealed in this chapter, only that he has one. All of the characters who were present at the first trial of Charles Darnay are now in St. Antoine (except for the inconsequential Mr. Stryver). Carton comments that "any one carried home by the crowd to-day may be condemned to-morrow," a reference to the treatment of Charles Darnay, that also makes a more general point about the fickleness of crowds, one of the continuing themes of *A Tale of Two Cities*.

We can see in this chapter how every minor plot development so far is going to tie into the main plot. We are left awaiting the final six chapters, wondering how all of these elements are going to fit together in the plot's resolution.

Study Questions

1. Who does Miss Pross see in the wine-shop?

2. What does Jerry Cruncher ask Solomon Pros, and what is this a reference to?

3. Who provides Jerry with an answer to his question?

4. What does Carton want with Barsad?

5. What do they discuss there?

6. What does Jerry Cruncher reveal about Roger Cly?

7. How does Barsad explain this?

8. To whom does Carton refer to in his comment about crowds and what is the point of this?

9. What does Barsad tell Carton after Carton questions Barsad's access to the prison?

10. How does this chapter end?

Answers

1. She sees her long-lost brother, Solomon.

2. He asks Pross what his name was back in England when he was a spy-witness at Charles Darnay's trial.

3. The just-arrived-in-France Sydney Carton states Barsad's name.

4. He wants Barsad to accompany him to Tellson's Bank.

5. They discuss why Carton has power over Barsad.

6. He reveals that Roger Cly was not in the coffin that Barsad claims he was in.

7. He says that Cly had to fake his death or risk being murdered by an unruly mob.

8. It refers to Charles Darnay's being carried home on the shoulders of a crowd, only to be arrested again.

9. He tells Carton that an escape is impossible.

10. It ends with Carton leading Barsad into a darkened room so that they can finish their negotiations in secret.

Suggested Essay Topics

1. Explain how the various subplots are becoming important to the action of the central story. Pay attention to Jerry Cruncher's "honest trade" as well as Sydney Carton's earlier behavior and keep in mind Barsad's previous actions.

2. Discuss the significance of Sydney Carton's comment about "dangerous times" and the nature of crowds. What does his comment about playing a "losing hand" foreshadow?

Chapter 9: The Game Made

Summary

This chapter begins with Mr. Lorry asking Jerry Cruncher, "What have you been, besides a messenger?" Cruncher explains, in his colloquial accent, just why he has sometimes been a grave robber. Lorry threatens to end his friendship with Cruncher; he reconsiders when Jerry tells him that it is only the odd jobs from Tellson's that prevent grave-robbing from being his full-time profession. Carton returns and tells Lorry, "If things should go ill with the prisoner, I have ensured access to him, once." Lorry does not see how this could help Darnay; Carton implores Lorry not to tell Lucie of these arrangements. Lorry swears to keep the secret; Carton thanks him and says, "She has such a strong attachment to you and reliance on you."

Lorry and Carton discuss Lorry's long life and his lifelong commitment to business. Lorry speaks of how pleasant memories long forgotten come back to him now that he is near the end of his life. Carton passes the wood-sawyer on the street and they have a discussion of the guillotine; the wood-sawyer is impressed that 63 people were beheaded that very day.

Carton then stops in at a chemist's shop and buys two "packets"; the chemist comments, "You will be careful to keep them separate, citizen? You know the consequences of mixing them?" Carton

wanders the street, thinking of his father's funeral long ago, and the words that were spoken there: "I am the resurrection and the life, saith the Lord: he that believeth in me, though he were dead, yet shall he live." Carton stands on a bridge and watches the current of the river, all the while repeating, "I am the resurrection."

The trial begins; the list of those who denounced Darnay is read: Ernest and Therese Defarge and Alexandre Manette. Dr. Manette insists that this is not true. Ernest Defarge then produces a paper that he says he found in Dr. Manette's former cell in the Bastille. The chapter ends with this paper about to be read.

Analysis

Mr. Lorry is angry with Jerry because he thinks that Jerry has caused Tellson's Bank harm. He is about to end their friendship but shows his human side when Jerry explains that grave-robbing was all he could do to supplement his income.

Sydney Carton's plan is still shrouded in mystery. Hints are given that it involves his own death, though: his conversation with Lorry about death, his remembrance of his father's funeral, his purchase of volatile chemicals, and his recitation of "I am the resurrection." Carton is comparing himself to Christ, and perhaps preparing a similar fate for himself.

We learn that Dr. Manette is the mysterious third voice that has denounced Darnay but are left waiting until the next chapter to find the substance of this denunciation.

Study Questions

1. Why is Mr. Lorry angry with Jerry Cruncher?

2. What deal has Sydney Carton worked out with Barsad?

3. What is Lorry's reaction to this?

4. Where does Carton go after he leaves Lorry?

5. What does he do there?

6. What does Carton do for the rest of the night?

7. What goes through his head during this long night?

8. Where had he first heard these words?

9. Who is the mysterious third person who has denounced Charles Darnay?

10. How has this denunciation come about?

Answers

1. Lorry feels that Cruncher has imposed on Tellson's Bank by being a grave-robber as well as an odd job man for the bank.

2. He has ensured access to Charles Darnay, once.

3. He says that this can do the prisoner no good.

4. He goes to a chemist's shop.

5. He buys two chemicals that are dangerous when mixed together.

6. He wanders the streets of Paris.

7. He keeps thinking, "I am the resurrection."

8. He first heard these words of the Lord at his father's funeral.

9. The mysterious third person is Alexandre Manette.

10. Ernest Defarge produces a paper that is said to hold this denunciation.

Suggested Essay Topics

1. Write an essay on Sydney Carton's behavior in this chapter. Why does it seem that he is preparing for his own death? What can be inferred about his plan from his behavior?

2. Examine Mr. Lorry's interactions in this chapter. Consider his discussion with both Jerry Cruncher and Sydney Carton. How do these conversations resolve previous thematic concerns? How do they help to move the plot forward?

Chapter 10: The Substance of the Shadow

Summary

Dr. Manette's letter is produced in this chapter. In it, he explains how he has come to be in prison. He writes that he keeps this letter in the wall of the chimney, in a place of concealment that he has dug out, hoping that "Some pitying hand may find it there, when I and my sorrows are dust."

Dr. Manette's story begins in December 1757. He is stopped on the street by a carriage. Two men insist that he enter the carriage as they have a patient who needs his attention. The men are armed; Dr. Manette enters their carriage. These two men take Dr. Manette to the patient: a beautiful 20-year-old woman, "in high fever," her arms bound with a gentleman's clothing, a portion of which bore the letter E. She is shrieking, over and over, "My husband, my father, my brother," and then counting to 12.

One of the two men (who are brothers) who had brought Dr. Manette to this place, the elder brother, indifferently tells Dr. Manette that there is another patient. The other patient is a 17-year-old "handsome peasant boy." His wound is a "sword-thrust" in the chest. Manette asks the elder brother how this has happened; the man replies that his brother was forced to duel this "common dog." He tells Manette this information without "pity, sorrow, or kindred humanity." The boy tells Dr. Manette that the woman is his sister.

The boy explains to Dr. Manette that one of these "noble" men had taken an interest in his sister. The man abused his class privilege and drove the woman's husband to his death. He died on his wife's bosom at the stroke of 12. The two brothers then took the woman away. The boy tracked them to the house they are now in. The boy falters in the telling of his story here; he condemns the "Marquis...to the last of (his) bad race" to answer for what he and his brother have done. The boy dies. The older brother then tells Dr. Manette that he must keep all of this secret in order to protect his brother. The woman lingers for a week and then dies. Dr. Manette notes that he never learned her family name. The brothers offer him money, which he refuses. Dr. Manette keeps their secret, only writing a letter to his minister, so that he can unburden his heart with the assurance that the minister will stay in his confidence.

Soon, a woman arrives at Dr. Manette's house; she presents herself as the wife of "Marquis St. Evremonde." Dr. Manette realizes that she is the wife of the elder brother. She wishes to make amends to the dead woman's younger sister for her family's behavior. She points to a small boy in her carriage and says she wishes to make atonement for "his sake." She calls the child "Charles." Later that night, a man shows up and arrests Dr. Manette in the presence of his servant, Ernest Defarge. Dr. Manette ends his letter by addressing the Evremonde family: "them and their descendants, to the last of their race...I denounce them to Heaven and to earth." The reading of this letter leads to Darnay's condemnation and a sentence of "Death within four-and-twenty hours!"

Analysis

This chapter explains the substance behind Dr. Manette's condemnation of the whole Evremonde family and, thus, Charles Darnay. The reading of this letter allows the reader to make some connections. The horrible sins of the family that Darnay spoke of with his uncle are presented here. We can now assume that Darnay's secret, revealed to Dr. Manette on the wedding night, was his family name. Dr. Manette has known all along that he has denounced the whole family, and his struggle to forgive Darnay can be seen as the cause of his many relapses into shoemaking.

While one mystery has been solved, Dickens presents another one. The family name of those wronged by the Evremondes is still not known to the reader. Also, we are not yet aware of Therese Defarge's reasons for denouncing Charles Darnay.

The behavior of the Evremonde family is the final, most chilling example of the horrible way in which the nobility treated the peasants.

Study Questions

1. What does this chapter consist of?

2. How do the two men who take Dr. Manette to the "patients" get him to enter the carriage?

3. Who are the two patients?

4. How has the boy received his wound?

5. What is this boy's fate?

6. What becomes of his sister?

7. What important fact does Dr. Manette not learn?

8. To whom does Dr. Manette confide his secret?

9. How does Dr. Manette learn the name of the two evil brothers?

10. What is the result of the reading of this letter?

Answers

1. The bulk of this chapter is a reproduction of the letter Dr. Manette wrote while he was imprisoned.

2. The two men are armed, so Dr. Manette has no choice but to go with them.

3. A young peasant boy with a wound in his chest and his 20-year-old sister who is "in high fever."

4. The younger of the two brothers has stabbed him.

5. He dies after denouncing the two men and their family name.

6. She dies a week later.

7. He does not learn the names of the brother and sister.

8. He writes a letter to his minister.

9. The wife of the elder brother comes to him, asking him to help her make atonement. She tells Dr. Manette their name.

10. Charles Darnay is condemned to die in 24 hours.

Suggested Essay Topics

1. Write an essay describing how the information learned in this chapter changes our perception of Dr. Manette. Does he seem like a stronger character now? Why or why not?

2. Examine what is revealed in this chapter about Charles

Darnay's family. How does this help to explain his renunciation of his family? What role does his mother play in all of this?

Chapter 11: Dusk
Chapter 12: Darkness

Summary

These chapters open with Lucie imploring the crowd that has gathered to let her embrace her husband one last time. They allow it; Darnay and Lucie say their farewells. Darnay is taken away and Lucie collapses at her father's feet. Sydney Carton carries her to a coach and then up to her apartment. There he sees Little Lucie, who says to him, "Now that you have come, I think…you will do

something to save Papa!" Carton kisses Lucie, says, "A life you love," and goes into the next room. Dr. Manette leaves to make a final attempt to save Darnay. Both Lorry and Carton state that they have no hope. Sydney Carton takes his leave and proceeds to the Defarges' wine-shop. He overhears Madame Defarge say that he looks like Evremonde. He also learns that Madame Defarge is the sister of the two who were so violently mistreated by the Evremondes. Madame Defarge wishes to condemn Dr. Manette and Lucie as relations of Evremonde/Defarge. Her husband thinks this is going too far, but she tells him, "Tell the wind and the fire where to stop; not me." Carton leaves and visits Mr. Lorry.

Dr. Manette comes home, looking for his shoemaking tools. He has lost all reason, and no one can restore him. He is "the exact figure that Defarge had had in keeping." Carton speaks with Lorry; he gives Lorry a certificate that allows Carton to leave France, asking Lorry to hold it for him until the next day. He also gives him a certificate that allows Dr. Manette and his daughter to leave. He then tells Lorry of Madame Defarge's plan to denounce Dr. Manette and Lucie. Carton tells Lorry to secure a coach for the next day at two o'clock. He tells Lorry to have Lucie and Dr. Manette in the coach and to wait for him before departing. Carton says to Lorry, "Wait for nothing but to have my place occupied, and then for England."

Analysis

This chapter helps to explain Madame Defarge's character. As the sister of those wronged by the Evremondes, she has a personal stake in the Revolution. These personal motivations are very ironic when one considers that Madame Defarge had earlier stated that personal concerns are of no importance to the Revolution. Her desire to see Darnay and his family dead is based on past injustice, and for the first time in the novel, it becomes possible to feel sympathy for Madame Defarge.

Dr. Manette's relapse shows that things have gotten nearly as bad as they can get. It is Little Lucie who offers a glimmer of hope with her faith that Sydney Carton will save her "Papa." We still do not know what Carton's plan is, but Little Lucie's confidence seems a hint that he will indeed save the day.

Study Questions

1. What does Lucie ask of the crowd at the trial?
2. Who helps Lucie when she faints?
3. What does Little Lucie say to Carton?
4. What happens to Dr. Manette in this chapter?
5. What does Carton learn about Madame Defarge while he is at the wine-shop?
6. What is ironic about this revelation?
7. What are Madame Defarge's plans for Dr. Manette and Lucie?
8. What does Carton tell Lorry to do?
9. What does Carton give to Lorry?
10. What is the final condition that Carton gives Lorry?

Answers

1. She asks them to let her touch her husband for one last time.
2. Sydney Carton helps Lucie.
3. She says that she knows Carton will save her father.
4. He relapses into his shoemaking ways of prison.
5. He learns that she is the sister of those who were wronged by the Evremondes.
6. It reveals that she had personal motives when she earlier stated that individuals do not matter in the revolution.
7. She plans to denounce both of them.
8. He tells Lorry to reserve a coach for two o'clock the next afternoon.
9. He gives him certificates that will allow Carton, Dr. Manette, and Lucie to leave France.
10. He tells Lorry, "Wait for nothing but to have my place occupied, and then to England!"

Suggested Essay Topics

1. How does Madame Defarge's revelation change our perception of her character? Can she be viewed with more sympathy now that her motivation has been revealed? Do her motives justify her behavior? Why or why not?

2. Write an essay about Sydney Carton's plan. Can it be inferred at this point of the novel? Could it have been inferred earlier? If so, does this point to a dramatic failing of the plot? Why or why not?

Chapter 13: Fifty-two

Summary

Fifty-two prisoners are awaiting the guillotine, "From the farmer of seventy…to the seamstress of twenty." Charles Darnay, after some deliberation, resigns himself to his fate and writes loving notes to Lucie, Dr. Manette, and Mr. Lorry; he never thinks of Sydney Carton, "never once." He falls asleep, knowing that he is to be executed at two o'clock the next day. A little after noon, Sydney Carton comes to his cell. Carton tells Darnay he comes with a "most earnest, pressing, and emphatic entreaty" from his wife. Carton insists that Darnay switch boots with him. Carton subtly passes his hand before Darnay's face, prompting Darnay to ask, "What vapour is that?" Carton tells him, "I am conscious of nothing." Carton then holds his fist under Darnay's nose; Darnay faints. Carton then switches clothes with Darnay and calls Barsad into the room. Carton tells Barsad to carry Darnay out under the claim that he is Carton, who "was weak and faint when you brought me in, and I am fainter now you take me out." This is done. A short time later a man leads Carton (as Evremonde) to a large, dark room." A condemned woman who was in La Force with Darnay addresses Carton in secret, "Are you dying for him?" He replies, "And his wife and child." Meanwhile, Lorry, Dr. Manette, Lucie, her daughter, and Darnay (disguised as Carton) are making their way through a checkpoint on the way to England, "with the whole wild night in pursuit of us; but so far…pursued by nothing else."

Analysis

Sydney Carton's plan is finally revealed. His physical similarity to Darnay allows for the plot to proceed as it does. This unbelievable coincidence makes it slightly difficult to fully believe what is taking place.

Carton uses the chemicals he purchased at the chemist's shop to knock Darnay out. His conversation with the condemned woman allows Carton to reveal that he is dying for Lucie and her child, as much as for Darnay. This conversation also portrays Carton as a hero for probably the first time in his life. He is making good on his earlier promise to Lucie that he would die for her. The fact that Darnay never once thinks of Carton illustrates that Carton is indeed taking Darnay's place for Lucie's sake. It is now apparent why Carton was comparing himself to Christ in Chapter 9. Little Lucie's confidence that Carton would save her father proves true. The only suspense now centers around whether or not Lucie and her family will safely escape France.

Study Questions

1. How many prisoners are awaiting their deaths?
2. What does Darnay do once he resigns himself to dying?
3. Who is not in Darnay's mind at all?
4. What does Sydney Carton tell Darnay?
5. How does Carton then proceed with his plan?
6. Whom does Carton call into the room to carry Darnay out?
7. Who does Carton meet as he awaits death?
8. What does this woman say to Carton?
9. What is Carton's reply?
10. How does this chapter end?

Answers

1. Fifty-two prisoners are awaiting death.
2. He sits down and writes letters to Lucie, Dr. Manette, and Mr. Lorry.
3. Darnay does not think of Sydney Carton.
4. He tells Darnay that he comes with an urgent entreaty from Darnay's wife.
5. He knocks Darnay out with the chemicals he purchased earlier.
6. Carton call John Barsad into the room.
7. He meets a woman who knew Darnay in the prison, La Force.
8. She asks him if he is dying for Evremonde (Darnay).

9. Carton replies that he is dying for him and his wife and child.

10. It ends with Lorry, Lucie, her daughter, Dr. Manette, and Darnay driving towards England.

Suggested Essay Topics

1. Write an essay about Sydney Carton's behavior in this chapter. What is his motivation for what he is doing? Think not only of his promise to Lucie but also of his reflections on the worthlessness of his own life.

2. What does the fact that Darnay does not once think about Carton reveal about the relationship between the two men? Does this affect our perception of what Carton does? In what way?

Chapter 14: The Knitting Done
Chapter 15: The Footsteps Die Out For Ever

Summary

While Carton is waiting to die, Madame Defarge is holding counsel with The Vengeance and Jacques Three. She is explaining to them that as a member of the Evremonde family, Lucie and her daughter must die. Madame Defarge does not trust her husband to join her in these feelings; she even thinks that he may warn Dr. Manette of these plans. For this reason, Madame Defarge says that the arrest of Lucie and her daughter must be carried out without delay. Madame Defarge also decides that Dr. Manette will be condemned with Lucie and the girl. Madame Defarge is described as "strong and fearless" and beautiful, but with a "hatred of a class" that makes her "absolutely without pity." Madame Defarge begins to make her way toward Lucie's apartment.

Meanwhile, Miss Pross and Jerry Cruncher are preparing to leave France. Cruncher repents for all his past sins, swearing that he will respect his wife and give up grave robbing. Miss Pross returns to the empty apartment just before Madame Defarge gets there. Madame Defarge realizes that Lucie and her family have

already left; she attempts to leave the apartment in order to pursue them. Miss Pross blocks the door. A struggle ensues; Madame Defarge gets shot by her own gun. The shot kills her and makes Miss Pross deaf.

The narrator then reflects on the revolution: "Sow the same seed of rapacious license and oppression over again, and it will surely yield the same fruit according to its kind." As he awaits the guillotine, Carton comforts the young woman who is to go before him. As she is led to the guillotine, Carton once again says, "I am the Resurrection..."

A Tale of Two Cities ends with the words that Sydney Carton may have been thinking as he was about to be beheaded. He looks into the future and thinks of Lucie and her family. He sees that he holds "sanctuary in their hearts." He sees a child named after him; he sees that his sacrifice will be remembered for generations to come. His final words and the final words of the novel, are: "It is a far, far better thing that I do, than I have ever done; it is a far, far better rest that I go to than I have ever known."

Analysis

These final chapters of *A Tale of Two Cities* tie up all the loose ends. An attempt is made to explain Madame Defarge's behavior; her death relieves the reader of having to decide whether or not she should be held accountable for her actions.

Jerry Cruncher repents for all of his sins and promises to be a better man when he gets back to England. Miss Pross loses her hearing as the depth of her loyalty to Lucie is revealed; her deafness makes her a martyr.

But it is Sydney Carton who is the true martyr. Carton looks to the future and sees that he will live on in the minds and hearts of Lucie and her family. This knowledge allows him to die at peace with himself. His final words show that he feels his selfless sacrifice is the only thing that could ever redeem his worthless life.

Study Questions

1. What does Madame Defarge decide at the beginning of the chapter?

2. Where does Madame Defarge then go?

3. What do we learn about Madame Defarge as she makes her way to Lucie's apartment?

4. Whom does Madame Defarge meet at Lucie's apartment?

5. What happens at the apartment?

6. What is the result of this struggle?

7. What does Jerry Cruncher do in this chapter?

8. What does Sydney Carton think of as he awaits the guillotine?

9. What are his thoughts regarding the future?

10. What are Sydney Carton's final thoughts regarding his life?

Answers

1. She decides that Lucie, her daughter, and Dr. Manette all must die.

2. She proceeds to Lucie's apartment.

3. We learn that she is a strong woman who has no pity because of the past treatment of her family.

4. Miss Pross is the only person there.

5. Madame Defarge tries to leave but Miss Pross blocks the door.

6. Madame Defarge is shot, she dies, and Miss Pross is rendered deaf.

7. He repents for all of his past sins.

8. He thinks of Lucie's family as it will be in the future.

9. Carton is comforted by the idea that he will always be remembered by them.

10. They are, "It is a far, far better thing that I do, than I have ever done; it is a far, far better rest that I go to than I have ever known."

Suggested Essay Topics

1. Write an essay about Madame Defarge. Can we feel any sympathy for her? What effect does her death have on any sympathetic feelings that we may have for her? How would her character seem different if she lived?

2. Examine Sydney Carton's final words. What do they say about his perception of his life? What do they reveal about his feelings concerning his act of sacrifice?

Sample Analytical Paper Topics

The following paper topics are based on the entire book. Following each topic is a thesis and sample outline. Use these as a starting point for your paper.

Topic #1

Write an analytical essay that examines how *A Tale of Two Cities* views different forms of government. Compare the English system with the pre- and post-Revolutionary systems in France. How are these systems alike? How are they different? What do these similarities and differences reveal about Dickens' opinions regarding governments?

Outline

I. Thesis Statement: *Throughout the novel, Dickens draws comparisons between the governments of England and France which reveal his opinions regarding governments.*

II. England

    A. Charles Darnay's trial for treason

        1. The prosecution's argument

        2. The defense's argument

    B. The verdict

        1. Darnay is acquitted

        2. The crowd is unhappy

    C. Roger Cly's "funeral"

        1. His conviction as a spy

        2. The mob's idea of justice

III. Pre-Revolutionary France

    A. Monsieur the Marquis

        1. His mistreatment of the peasants

        2. His argument with Charles Darnay about class

            a. Darnay's opinion

            b. The Marquis' opinion

    B. Dr. Manette's imprisonment

        1. Reason he was imprisoned

        2. Length of his incarceration

IV. Post-Revolutionary France

    A. Charles Darnay's arrest and imprisonment

        1. Reason for arrest

        2. Conditions in prison

    B. Darnay's first trial

        1. Argument of prosecution

        2. Argument in Darnay's defense

        3. Result of trial

    C. Darnay's second trial

        1. Reason for arrest

        2. Argument of prosecution

        3. Argument in defense

        4. Result of trial

    D. Punishment in Post-Revolutionary France

        1. Prison sentences

        2. Beheadings

Topic #2

Write an essay that examines the roles that women play in the novel. Compare and contrast Lucie Manette and Therese Defarge. What do their respective behaviors reveal about Victorian ideals?

Outline

I. Thesis Statement: *The two significant women characters in the novel, Lucie Manette and Therese Defarge, represent contrasting ideas about the role of women in Victorian society.*

II. Lucie Manette

    A. Relations to men

        1. Her father

        2. Jarvis Lorry

        3. Charles Darnay

    B. Moral behavior

        1. Displays of compassion

        2. Examples of selfless behavior

    C. Role in the Revolution

        1. Concern for the individual

        2. Ability to think of the Revolution in an impersonal manner

III. Therese Defarge

    A. Relations to men

        1. Ernest Defarge

        2. Charles Darnay

        3. The "Jacques"

    B. Immoral behavior

        1. Denunciation of Darnay

        2. Murder of Foulon

      3. Leader of Revolution

   C. Role in Revolution

      1. Knitting death register

      2. Leading women in riots

      3. Organizing resistance to government

IV. Manner of presentation of women

   A. Defined through men

      1. Lucie defined through Darnay

      2. Lucie defined through her father

      3. Therese Defarge in opposition to her husband

   B. Victorian ideals as displayed by Lucie

      1. Passivity

      2. Reliance on men

   C. The antithesis of Victorian ideals as manifested in Therese Defarge

      1. Violence

      2. Independence

      3. Madness/passion

Topic #3

Write an analytical essay that explores the role of crowds in *A Tale of Two Cities*. Why are mobs violent by definition? Do crowds serve any "good" purpose in the novel? Examine both the actions of mobs and the narrator's comments about mob mentality.

Outline

I. Thesis Statement: *The nature of crowds and mobs is a significant theme throughout* A Tale of Two Cities.

II. Mobs at trials

   A. Darnay's trial in England

        1.   Comments crowd makes

        2.   Narrator's comment regarding crowd

    B. Darnay's trials in France

        1.   Fickleness of crowd at Darnay's first trial

            a.   Hope that Darnay will be hanged

            b.   Cheers at his acquittal

        2.   Ruthlessness of crowd at second trial

            a.   Elation at Darnay's death-sentence

            b.   Paradox of letting Darnay hug his wife

III. Mobs in the Revolution

    A. The storming of the Bastille

        1.   Peasants gain power through sheer numbers

        2.   Manipulation of mobs by the Defarges

    B. The crowd gathered at the grindstone

        1.   Description of crowd

        2.   Lorry's refusal to let the Manettes look out the window

    C. Vastness of crowds at public executions

        1.   Entertainment value of the guillotine

        2.   Blood-lust satisfied

SECTION SIX

Bibliography

Quotations from the text are based on the following edition:

Dickens, Charles. *A Tale of Two Cities*. New York: Signet Classic/ Penguin Books USA, 1980.

Introducing...

MAXnotes

A's Literature Study Guides

notes™ offer a fresh look at masterpieces of literature, presented in a lively nteresting fashion. **MAXnotes**™ offer the essentials of what you should know t the work, including outlines, explanations and discussions of the plot, acter lists, analyses, and historical context. **MAXnotes**™ are designed to help hink independently about literary works by raising various issues and thought-oking ideas and questions. Written by literary experts who currently teach the ct, **MAXnotes**™ enhance your understanding and enjoyment of the work.

Available **MAXnotes**™ include the following:

al Farm	Huckleberry Finn	Of Mice and Men
vulf	I Know Why the	The Odyssey
Canterbury Tales	Caged Bird Sings	Paradise Lost
h of a Salesman	The Iliad	Plato's Republic
e Comedy I-Inferno	Julius Caesar	A Raisin in the Sun
with the Wind	King Lear	Romeo and Juliet
Grapes of Wrath	Les Misérables	The Scarlet Letter
t Expectations	Macbeth	A Tale of Two Cities
Great Gatsby	Moby Dick	To Kill a Mockingbird
let	1984	

ESEARCH & EDUCATION ASSOCIATION
Ethel Road W. • Piscataway, New Jersey 08854
ione: (908) 819-8880

Please send me more information about MAXnotes™.

ne _____

dress _____

 _____ State _____ Zip _____